LIZZIE BORDEN

Discover More of History's Worst

— HISTORY'S WORST —

LIZZIE BORDEN

BY **MICHAEL BURGAN**

Aladdin

New York   London   Toronto   Sydney   New Delhi

ALADDIN

An imprint of Simon & Schuster Children's Publishing Division

1230 Avenue of the Americas, New York, New York 10020

First Aladdin paperback edition October 2018

Text copyright © 2018 by Simon & Schuster, Inc.

Cover illustration copyright © 2018 by Matt Rockefeller

Also available in an Aladdin hardcover edition.

All rights reserved, including the right of reproduction in whole or in part in any form.

ALADDIN and related logo are registered trademarks of Simon & Schuster, Inc.

For information about special discounts for bulk purchases, please contact Simon & Schuster Special Sales at 1-866-506-1949 or business@simonandschuster.com.

The Simon & Schuster Speakers Bureau can bring authors to your live event.

For more information or to book an event contact the Simon & Schuster Speakers Bureau at 1-866-248-3049 or visit our website at www.simonspeakers.com.

Designed by Nina Simoneaux

The text of this book was set in Adobe Caslon Pro.

Manufactured in the United States of America 0818 OFF

2 4 6 8 10 9 7 5 3 1

Library of Congress Control Number 2017955442

ISBN 978-1-4814-9652-0 (hc)

ISBN 978-1-4814-9651-3 (pbk)

ISBN 978-1-4814-9653-7 (eBook)

To my many nieces and nephews,

my most faithful readers

CONTENTS

1

MURDER COMES TO FALL RIVER

Ready for his day, Andrew J. Borden left his house around nine a.m. and headed to the business district of Fall River, Massachusetts, a city he had called home his entire life. He had taken this morning stroll for years. He had no idea that this would be the last time he'd do it.

The Borden name was well known in this manufacturing city along the Quequechan River. Andrew's ancestor Richard Borden had settled in Rhode Island during the 1630s, and other relatives then moved into nearby Fall River. Some of the Bordens became important business owners and leaders of the community. One distant relative of Andrew's was president of the Fall River Railroad, while another ran the local ironworks. Those Bordens and their closest family members were some of the richest people in town.

Andrew, though, came from a much simpler background. He had trained as a carpenter before going into the furniture business. Over the years, he became a successful businessman and investor. One local resident described him as "just and honest" but also "hard, stern, and puritanical."[1] Despite making plenty of money from his business dealings, Borden didn't like to spend it. It was said that Borden boasted he had never foolishly spent a single dollar. Even with his success, he chose to live with his family on Second Street rather than in the neighborhood known as the Hill, the most fashionable part of the city. Still, the Borden home was comfortable, and the family's neighbors included doctors and other professionals. Borden saw no need to show off his wealth by moving to a larger, fancier home. Besides, living at 92 Second Street gave him an easy walk into town.

When Borden set out on the morning of Thursday, August 4, 1892, he wasn't feeling so well. Two days earlier he had come down with an upset stomach, most likely from a case of food poisoning. The family had eaten some leftovers that had gone bad in the summer humidity. This day was already starting out as another muggy one.

As he ran his errands, Borden passed a building he owned that had his name prominently displayed on the front. He then stopped in briefly at the National Union Bank, where he was president. He continued on to the post office before heading to another bank; for that one, he served on the board of directors. Going to the banks to deposit a check or carry out some other business was almost a daily ritual for Borden. He also stopped to chat with people on the street. That day he talked with Jonathan Clegg, a store owner who rented space from him. Borden also went to one of his properties where workmen were making repairs. But at least one person Borden met that day noticed that the businessman was still under the weather. The lingering queasiness in his stomach may have led Borden to cut short his daily rounds and head back home.

Andrew Borden lived with his wife, Abby, and his adult daughters, Emma and Lizzie, the children from his first marriage. The family had had a houseguest the night of August 3: John Morse, Mr. Borden's brother-in-law from his first marriage. Morse and Borden often talked business. That morning the two men and Mrs. Borden had breakfast together; then Morse left the house shortly before Borden, though he expected to return for dinner. Emma was away visiting friends, so just Lizzie, Mrs. Borden, and the housekeeper, Bridget, were home when Mr. Borden returned.

———— ❧ ————

THE FIRST BLOODY BODY

HE WENT FIRST to the side door and, finding it locked, went next to the front door. That door was locked too, and he fumbled a bit with his keys. Inside, Bridget heard him at the door and came over to let him in. She was surprised to find it locked and let out a little cry of frustration as she tried to open it. Lizzie was upstairs at the time, by the front stairs, and she laughed as she heard Bridget's troubles with the door.

Lizzie soon came down to greet her father. He sat in the dining room, reading, and she asked if he had any mail for her. He said no. Then Lizzie told her father that Mrs. Borden was not home after all. Someone had come to the door earlier in the morning with a note that asked Abby to go visit a sick friend.

As she did her chores, Bridget saw Mr. Borden walking through the house before he finally settled down in the sitting room to read the newspaper. In the dining room, Lizzie had set up an ironing board to iron handkerchiefs—one household task she always did herself. Thanks to her father's money, Lizzie didn't have to work. She could sleep late, as she had that morning, and generally avoid doing much housework. Cleaning their own rooms was about all Lizzie and her sister regularly did. Taking a break from her ironing, Lizzie went into the kitchen and mentioned to Bridget that Mrs. Borden had gone out. Then the two young women discussed a sale at a local store.

By now, Mr. Borden had stretched out his tall, thin body on the sofa in the sitting room. When Lizzie saw him, he had stopped reading and was simply resting. Lizzie then went outside for a few minutes. Meanwhile, Bridget went upstairs to take a break from her chores. She heard a bell ringing in the distance at city hall, signaling that it was eleven o'clock. A few minutes later Bridget heard Lizzie yelling her name from downstairs, saying, "Come down quick. Father's dead. Somebody came in and killed him."[2] Later, though, Lizzie said that in that moment, she wasn't sure whether he was dead, but she was "so frightened and horrified" by what she saw.[3]

Bridget rushed down the stairs and found Lizzie standing by the bloody body of Andrew Borden. But he was not merely bloody—his head and face had been hacked with an ax, leaving a hole in his skull and deep cuts that had splattered the walls with blood. One eyeball had been sliced in half. "Go for Dr. Bowen," Lizzie ordered, and Bridget ran out to get the doctor, who lived across the street.[4]

As Bridget dashed across the street to look for Dr. Bowen, Adelaide Churchill was returning from grocery shopping. She lived next to the Bordens. She saw Bridget leave the doctor's house alone and head back home. The neighbor noticed the housekeeper's frightened look. Churchill then went inside to put away her groceries. Looking through a window, she saw Lizzie outside by the side door. She, too, looked frightened or upset. Opening the window, Churchill asked Lizzie if something was wrong. Lizzie replied, "Oh, Mrs. Churchill, do come over; somebody has killed father."[5]

Churchill quickly ran over. Bridget was gone again, as Lizzie had sent her to get Alice Russell, one of her friends. Churchill arrived to see Lizzie sitting on a step of the house's back stairs. She explained that she had been in the barn, heard a noise, and come into the house to find her father's mutilated body. Churchill asked where Mrs. Borden was, and Lizzie said, "I don't know where Mrs. Borden is. I think she is out, but I wish you would look."[6] Lizzie explained again about the note Abby Borden had received that morning, and while she assumed her stepmother had gone out, she didn't know for sure if she had returned. Lizzie said she might have heard her come in. If Abby had returned, she might have suffered the same bloody fate as Mr. Borden.

ANOTHER GRUESOME DISCOVERY

SINCE DR. BOWEN wasn't home, Lizzie asked Churchill to go search for another doctor. The neighbor headed out, leaving Lizzie alone at the crime scene, but not for long. Dr. Bowen came home and his wife told him about trouble at the Borden residence. He went over and found Lizzie in the hall. By then, both Bridget and Churchill had returned. Lizzie explained that her father had been killed. Bowen asked if she had seen anyone, and Lizzie said no. After Bowen announced that Mr. Borden was indeed dead, Lizzie asked him to send a telegraph to her sister Emma to tell her what had happened. While the doctor was away, Lizzie once again said that Mrs. Borden could be in the house too. Bridget and Churchill went upstairs—Bridget refused to go alone—and the two made a gruesome discovery in the guest bedroom. Even before they reached the top of the stairs, they could see a body lying under the bed. Without looking any further, Churchill was sure it was the dead body of Abby Borden, and she hurried back down the stairs, filled with fear. As a local newspaper later reported the scene, Abby "had died evidently where she had been struck, for her life blood formed a ghastly clot on the carpet."[7]

Fall River police soon arrived at the home, and as the day went on, Lizzie answered a barrage of questions from the officers investigating the crime. Her friend Alice Russell was there for much of the time, and the two women presented very different images. Officer Philip Harrington wrote in his notes that Russell was "very pale, and much agitated, which she showed by short sharp breathing and wringing her hands." Lizzie, on the other hand, "talked in the most calm and collected manner; her whole bearing was most remarkable under the circumstances." At one point, Harrington offered to wait till the next day to question Lizzie further, when she might be less upset. Lizzie replied, "No, I can tell you all I know now just as well as any other time." The exchange with Lizzie did not sit well with Harrington. As he wrote in his notes, "I don't like that girl."[8]

By nightfall, Second Street was still crowded with local people seeking more information about the horrible crime. Newspapers in and around Fall River reported what little was known at the time, including rumors that a Portuguese man who worked on a farm Andrew Borden owned was a suspect. The *Boston Advertiser* played up the gory nature of the murders, reporting that the Bordens' heads were "chopped to pieces by repeated and fiendish blows with an axe." The paper wrote that some twelve hours after the bodies were first discovered, "the police and the people are in just as utter ignorance as they were when it was first noised abroad this noon."[9]

Within a few days, however, the police had a suspect in the grisly murders: Lizzie Borden. Her parents' murders and then her trial captivated the country. Some people couldn't imagine that a young woman from a wealthy and respectable family could commit such a crime. Others, though, saw Lizzie as cool and calculating—and able to kill in cold blood. Here is her story.

THE FAMOUS RHYME

More than 120 years after the murder of Andrew and Abby Borden, the most some people know about the case comes from a simple rhyme:

> *Lizzie Borden took an axe*
> *And gave her mother forty whacks,*
> *When she saw what she had done,*
> *She gave her father forty-one.*

The little poem has been called a nursery rhyme and a jump-rope song, and it seems children began reciting it not long after the crime. The rhyme, though, is not historically accurate, as the killer used only twenty-nine blows of the murder weapon, not the eighty-one mentioned. The rhyme has had several variations, as explained by Olive Woolley Burt in her 1958 book, *American Murder Ballads*. In one version, after Lizzie delivered the first forty whacks, she "stood behind the door, and gave her father forty more." Another version goes:

> *Andrew Borden, he is dead;*
> *Lizzie hit him on the head.*
> *Lizzie killed her mother, too—*
> *What a horrid thing for Liz to do!*[10]

2

FALL RIVER AND THE BORDENS

The city shocked by the news of Andrew and Abby Borden's gruesome murders was a thriving one in 1892, with population of about seventy-five thousand. Fall River was named for the falling waters of the Quequechan River, with its eight separate falls powering the town's first textile mills. Later, steam engines fed with coal spun the spindles that held the yarn that factory workers turned into cloth. The thousands of spindles in the mills led to Fall River's nickname: the Spindle

City. During Lizzie Borden's life, Fall River became America's leading textile city, and local companies shipped their products all over the world.

The town of Fall River was first established in 1803, and members of the extended Borden family played a part. The first town meeting was held in the home of Louisa Borden, and two other Bordens served on a committee to handle the town's affairs. When Andrew J. Borden was born in 1822, Fall River had about three hundred families, and farming was still important for many people in and around the town. His father, Abraham, was not part of one of the wealthy Borden families. At times he held different jobs, including selling fish and working as a gardener. The town was just then beginning its days as a manufacturing center, with the Fall River Iron Works opening the year before Andrew was born. Other factories that made cloth soon followed. One of the mills, according to a 1911 history of the city, "was so great a wonder that people came from far and near to see it, for its size was remarkable in mill construction."[11]

While Andrew's family lived a simple life, the boy experienced several exciting events. When he was nine, his aunt discovered a human skeleton surrounded by some arrowheads and a few metal objects. Some people thought it could have been the remains of a Viking, but the bones most likely came from a local Native American. The next year, all of Fall River buzzed with the discovery of a dead woman hanging from a pole. She was a weaver at one of the mills. A local minister was suspected of the crime, and news of it spread across the country—just as Andrew's own murder later spurred widespread fascination.

Andrew Borden also experienced the Great Fire of 1843, which was supposedly started by local boys beginning their Fourth of July celebration two days early. Shifting winds probably prevented the blaze from raging across the whole town, but it still destroyed almost two hundred buildings. Residents quickly rebuilt, and Fall River continued to grow.

During these years, Andrew Borden received some schooling and also learned carpentry and worked as a cabinetmaker. He helped build the new city hall. Then he, his father, and his friend William Almy bought a building in the center of town. In March 1845 Andrew Borden and Almy went into business together at the site, making furniture. Over time, the partners expanded into making coffins and became undertakers, arranging funerals for local residents. Later they sold coffins made by other manufacturers, and an ad they ran in the newspaper described one casket with a glass top, offering "a view of the entire body after . . . enclosed."[12]

THE EMBALMING IN THE BASEMENT?

Undertaking—preparing a body for burial—was much different in Andrew Borden's day than it is today. While one undertaker did develop chemicals to embalm, or preserve, the body, many simply used chunks of ice for that purpose. Borden and William Almy didn't seem to have any particular skills as embalmers. Their services consisted of providing a casket, holding a wake for the surviving relatives, and carrying the coffin to the cemetery. In the years after Borden's death, stories began to circulate around Fall River about how he had conducted his funeral business. One of them was still being reported during the 1960s, in Victoria Lincoln's book *A Private Disgrace: Lizzie Borden by Daylight*. Lincoln grew up in Fall River and her parents had known Andrew and Abby Borden. Lincoln wrote that people in the city "used to enjoy saying that he cut off the feet of corpses so that he could cram them into undersized coffins that he got cheap."[13] The myth tied into Borden's reputation for being tight with money. And given the bloody nature of his own death, the myth seemed to suggest that he might have gotten what he had coming.

Later in 1845 Andrew married Sarah Morse. She was a seamstress, and little is known about her, though she did pose for two pictures that survive today. During the first few years of his marriage, Andrew Borden focused on growing his business rather than starting a family, and he and his partner Almy did well. Finally, in 1851, he and Sarah had their first child, a daughter they named Emma.

THE NEW MRS. BORDEN

THE BORDENS LIVED for a time with Andrew's father on Ferry Street, then moved to another house the Borden family owned on that street. In 1856 Andrew and Sarah had a second daughter, Alice, but she died of illness before her second birthday. Then, in 1860, the Bordens had their third and last child: Lizzie Andrew. Before Lizzie's third birthday, Sarah Borden died, leaving Andrew to raise his two daughters on his own. Before she died, Emma later recalled, her mother told her to "always watch over 'baby' Lizzie."[14]

Sometime after this, Andrew Borden met Abby Gray in church. Abby's family had also gone through upheaval during the early 1860s. Her mother died in 1860, and her father soon remarried and had a child. Abby was thirty-seven years old and still living at home at the time, and by the standards of the day she was considered a spinster—an older woman who had not and might never marry. When Andrew Borden proposed in 1865, she accepted. Some people have wondered if the couple was really in love, noting that Andrew didn't wear a wedding ring. Perhaps he thought his children needed a mother. But no one disputed that Abby was a kind woman, and some noted that she tried to have a good relationship with her stepdaughters.

Lizzie grew up on Ferry Street, which was home to mill

workers and craftspeople, though both wealthier and poorer families lived on nearby streets. She walked to her elementary school, which, given Fall River's fast growth, probably had overcrowded classrooms. Her neighborhood reflected the ethnic diversity of the city. Fall River was founded by Yankees—Protestants with roots in England who had settled in New England decades or even centuries before. Many of the newcomers, though, came from Ireland, the French-speaking part of Canada, and Portuguese islands called the Azores. Most belonged to the Roman Catholic Church. The French Canadians, in particular, came to dominate the city's working class. Yankee families, however, typically saw themselves as forming a higher social class than the more recent Catholic arrivals.

Lizzie received most of her schooling at the Morgan Street School, which she attended from grades three through eight. One person who had a good chance to observe Lizzie and her family during some of those years was Horace Benson. He rented a room in a house on Second Street, where the Bordens had moved to in 1872, and he was also the principal of the Morgan Street School. Years later Benson recalled Lizzie as an "average scholar, neither being exceptionally smart, nor noticeably dull." He, like others who knew Lizzie then, also commented on her "varying moods."[15] Some students of the Borden case wonder if she might have had a touch of depression or mental illness that ran in her family.

After the Borden murders, a few people noted that Sarah Borden's family had several members that some Fall River residents considered odd or perhaps emotionally unstable. Sarah herself was said to have a bad temper. One resident went so far as to say that some members of the Morse family "are worse than insane."[16] At least one other Fall River resident, however, rejected the idea that either the Borden or Morse families had been touched by mental illness.

Principal Benson also seemed to have some knowledge of Lizzie and Emma's relationship with their stepmother. Benson said that Abby Borden tried but failed to win her new daughters' love, and that Lizzie "was never fond of her . . . and in many ways showed her dislike of her father's second wife."[17] Instead Lizzie was close to her older sister, who seemed to have taken to heart their mother's dying words to watch over Lizzie. The two sisters lived together for decades. The only time Emma left the Borden home for any length of time was in 1867 and 1868, when she attended college in Norton, Massachusetts. As Lizzie later said, Abby had never really felt like a mother to her in many ways. If she had a problem, she explained, "I always went to my sister because she was older and had the care of me after my mother died."[18]

HIGH SCHOOL YEARS

LIZZIE BORDEN ENTERED high school in 1875. As other students did at the time, she first had to take an exam to prove she was qualified. Although not extremely popular with other students, she did have several close friends. She and her sister also seemed to have a flair for fashion, as photos of them from their teenage years show. They wore stylish clothes, and Emma had her hair fancily done. The pictures suggest that while Mr. Borden could be cheap, he was willing to spend some money on his daughters.

Money seemed to be an issue at times between the daughters and their father. While their Second Street home was comfortable, the girls would have preferred to live in the much nicer part of Fall River, on the Hill. And whatever fine things their father bought them, they still felt somewhat cheated. As one resident recalled, they "saw girls whose fathers' resources were not one-tenth of theirs lapped in luxuries which were denied them."[19]

The family house did have what were then modern conveniences. It had central heating, powered by a coal-burning furnace, and the house was connected to the city water supply. The two sinks, though, had only cold water. At a time when many families still used outhouses, the Bordens also had a flush toilet, though it was in the basement, two floors below the family's bedrooms. That meant that at night, the family sometimes used pots or pails to hold their waste, rather than making the trip downstairs. In what some people took as another example of Andrew Borden's cheapness, he sometimes stocked the toilet with old newspapers rather than softer paper.

Lizzie spent just two years in high school, and why she left before graduating is a mystery. Little evidence exists to suggest what Lizzie was like during those years, though the diary of one of her classmates offers some glimpses. Louisa "Lulie" Stillwell was the daughter of a successful merchant and almost two years older than Lizzie. Lulie's uncle and Andrew Borden were good friends. While in high school, the two girls sometimes walked home together, and Lulie sometimes visited the Borden home. In her diary, Lulie wrote about visiting a farm the Bordens owned in nearby Swansea. She noted several times when Lizzie was "rather blue" and "real miserable," which added to the image of her unhappiness.[20]

3

THE BORDEN SISTERS AND ABBY

During Lizzie's teen years, Andrew Borden continued to do well in business. That was when he bought his first farmland outside the city, and he continued to buy more in the years to come. In 1878 Borden sold his interest in the company he owned with William Almy, though he still owned a share of the building. Borden would come to own other commercial space in town that he rented to various businesses. The most prominent was a three-story brick-and-iron building named after him, which Borden constructed in 1889.

After Lizzie cut short her schooling, she left behind few clues about what she did with her time. There's no evidence that she worked outside the house or that she dated. After the murders, an unnamed relative told a reporter from the *Fall River Herald* that Mr. Borden never prevented either of his daughters from dating, as long as the men were respectable. But the person also went on to say that Lizzie had a "haughty and cold nature . . . [that] was repellant to some."[21] Emma, too, did not work, though like many ladies of the era, she joined several clubs. One of them was the Troy Book Club. Members, almost all women, collected money to buy books, which they then took turns reading. The books included popular novels of the day and biographies. Emma also joined the Fall River Women's Union. Its members, from some of the city's wealthiest families, sought to help women in Fall River who had to work. One effort was to provide housing for single working women. Later, in 1891, Lizzie also briefly joined the organization.

By that time, Lizzie had joined several other groups that tried to help people in Fall River. In 1887 she became an official member of the Central Congregational Church. Congregational churches across New England traced their roots to the Puritans, who had come to America from England during the 1630s and after. Respectable Yankee families in Fall River, like the Bordens, belonged to one of two Congregational churches in the city. Andrew Borden had been a member of Central Church since 1850.

As a member of Central Church, Lizzie taught Sunday school and volunteered for the Young People's Society of Christian Endeavor. More commonly called the Christian Endeavor Society, the group was formed in 1881 by a Congregational minister from Maine. Young people from different Protestant faiths came together to express their belief in Jesus Christ and try to help others. The society spread across the United States and into several foreign countries.

Charles Henry Wells, the son of a friend of Mr. Borden's, also was active at Central Church and noticed Lizzie's devotion to her faith. He wrote in his diary that of all the young people in the society, "there was not one who had seemed a more devoted member" than Lizzie.[22] She also volunteered for the local hospital and a group that provided meals to the poor. She was active with the Young Women's Christian Temperance Union. That organization encouraged others not to drink alcohol and hoped to make it illegal.

Through her religious and charitable activities, Lizzie became friendly with a group of young women. One of them had access to a cottage in Marion, Massachusetts, a village east of Fall River. On one visit there, Lizzie seemed to once again show signs of the moodiness or depression others seemed to detect. She told her friend Alice Russell that she noticed the feelings herself and had experienced them at the Marion cottage. "The girls were laughing and talking and having a good time, and this feeling came over me, and one of them spoke and said, 'Lizzie, why don't you talk?'"[23]

Despite any sadness she felt on that trip, Lizzie seemed to enjoy her friends and their social outings. And in 1890 she traveled with some young women from Fall River to Europe. They made what was called the grand tour, when the children of well-off families visited Europe's most famous buildings and admired its greatest art. The ladies went to Ireland, Great

Britain, Germany, Switzerland, Italy, and France. Along the way, Lizzie bought souvenir photos of the places she visited. When she returned home, she carefully arranged the photos in several albums so she could turn to the images and relive her trip.

On the way home, however, Lizzie didn't seem to look forward to returning to 92 Second Street. She shared a cabin on the ocean crossing with Anna Borden, a distant cousin. Anna later related that Lizzie had enjoyed such a happy summer in Europe, but now she "regretted the necessity of returning . . . because the home she was about to return to was such an unhappy home."[24]

Anna Borden never explained whether Lizzie gave details about what she meant. But the unhappiness may have stemmed from an incident three years before that pitted Lizzie and her sister against their stepmother.

FAMILY CONFLICT

IN 1887 ABBY Borden's half sister, Sarah Whitehead, faced a problem. She and her mother—Abby's stepmother, Jane Gray—each owned half the house they shared on Fourth Street. Mrs. Gray wanted to sell her interest in the house, and Sarah couldn't afford to pay her mother what it was worth. Fearing she might lose the house altogether, Sarah asked Abby if the Bordens could help her. Andrew Borden agreed to give Abby $1,500 so she could buy her stepmother's interest in the house and make sure it stayed in the family.

When Emma and Lizzie heard about this arrangement, they were not happy. Emma thought that if their father was going to give Abby property, she and Lizzie should get some too. Lizzie felt the same way. She heard about the house deal from people outside the family, and she confronted her stepmother about it and told her that "what he did for her, he ought to do for his own children."[25]

To satisfy his daughters, Andrew Borden sold them the house that had been their grandfather's on Ferry Street. The price: one dollar. It was valued at about $3,000, the same as the house that Abby Borden now partially owned. Later Mr. Borden bought the Ferry Street property back from Emma and Lizzie for $5,000.

Although Lizzie and Emma got the property they wanted,

the ordeal left Lizzie feeling bitter. She was sure that Abby had persuaded Mr. Borden to buy the half share in the Fourth Street home. Around this time, Lizzie almost completely stopped calling Abby "mother." Instead she began calling her stepmother "Mrs. Borden." Lizzie and Emma also started to ignore Abby's half sister Sarah when they saw her on the street, and Mrs. Gray, Abby's stepmother, reported that she rarely visited the Bordens because Emma and Lizzie treated her rudely too.

In one sense, it seemed that Mr. Borden tried to treat his second wife and his daughters equally. Each of the three women received an allowance of four dollars per week. But while Emma and Lizzie could spend their money as they chose, Abby could not spend her allowance on herself. Some of her four dollars had to go toward household expenses, such as curtains and towels. And while Abby had to manage the housekeeper and generally take care of the house, Lizzie and Emma had few household responsibilities. As Emma explained, they did what they chose to do "as we felt, if we wanted to, we did."[26]

Over time, Andrew seemed to sense the growing tension between his daughters and his wife. One incident in 1891 may have reflected his feelings. In June he and Abby went to the Swansea farm, while Lizzie, Emma, and the maid Bridget remained in Fall River. On the twenty-fourth, someone entered the Borden house while the three women were there and snuck into Abby's room. There, the thief stole some jewelry. In another room, the intruder broke into Mr. Borden's desk and stole some money and tickets used to ride the local streetcars.

Mr. Borden discovered and reported the burglary after returning from Swansea. The only clue was a nail that Lizzie found in the keyhole of a bedroom door. The police also kept an eye on the streetcars, in case the thief tried to use the tickets. As the investigation went on, Mr. Borden told a police captain, "I am afraid the police will not be able to find the real thief."[27] He told the police to drop the case. And, according to Lizzie's friend Alice Russell, he instructed his daughters not to talk about the burglary. The family became more careful to lock all the doors in the house.

The incident has raised questions for students of the Borden murders. Why would a thief risk entering a house that might be occupied and take only items on the second floor, far from the doors that led outside? How could the intruder escape detection by the three women at home? And why did Mr. Borden feel the police would never find the criminal? Historian Joseph A. Conforti has argued that perhaps Andrew suspected who the thief was: Lizzie. Her anger and jealousy toward her stepmother, Conforti believes, led Lizzie to commit the crime. And some Borden scholars have suggested that Lizzie was a kleptomaniac, meaning she was driven to steal, even if she didn't need what she took.

As with many theories about Lizzie Borden, there is no proof that she stole the money and jewelry. But by the next year, there were clear signs that relations between the Borden family members were not always good. That spring Lizzie wanted a new cloak and went to see Hannah Gifford, a local clothes maker. Gifford referred to Abby Borden as Lizzie's mother, which angered Lizzie. "Don't say that to me, for she is a mean good for nothing." Gifford replied, "Oh, Lizzie, you don't mean that?" Lizzie said she did, and that she tried to have as little to do with Abby as she could. "I stay in my room most of the time," Lizzie told the dressmaker, and added that both she and Emma avoided eating dinner with their parents.[28]

The strains in family relations increased over the summer. Without revealing details, Andrew Borden told someone that he and Abby would not be taking a vacation at the Swansea farm because "his family affairs were such this summer that he would not be able to go."[29] In July, Emma and Lizzie went on their own vacations without their parents. Lizzie spent a few days in New Bedford, while Emma went to visit a friend in Fairhaven. Lizzie stopped by Marion, too, and visited her sister at Fairhaven before returning to Fall River. Her friends staying at the Marion cottage wanted Lizzie to stay longer, but she had work to do for the Christian Endeavor Society and needed to be home on Sunday, August 1. Lizzie also might have wanted to keep her father company, as Abby Borden planned to go to the Swansea farm with a friend. As it turned out, the friend couldn't go, so Abby stayed in Fall River. As August began, Lizzie was home with her parents for what would become the family's most horrible days.

4

GROWING FEARS AND
GRUESOME MURDERS

On Tuesday evening, August 2, Bridget Sullivan prepared the Bordens' last meal of the day. At lunch, she had fried some fresh swordfish, and now the family would have the leftovers for dinner, along with some bread, tea, cake, and cookies. The meal, though, did not sit well with Abby and Andrew. During the night, both became sick and vomited in a pail they kept in their bedroom. Lizzie heard them stirring in the room and asked if everything was all right, and they said yes.

The fish seemed to be the likely cause of the Bordens' illness. In the days before homes had refrigerators, meat or fish could easily spoil on summer days. Abby Borden, though, was worried. Sometime between seven and eight a.m. on Wednesday, August 3, she visited her neighbor, Dr. Seabury Bowen, and said she feared she had been poisoned. She told the doctor that she had not had any of the fish, just some bread and cake. She explained how she and Andrew had started vomiting before midnight, and Lizzie seemed to be sick after that, though not as badly as her parents. Sitting in Dr. Bowen's office, Abby almost got sick again. Dr. Bowen told her to take something to get the foul taste out of her mouth and then sent her home, unconcerned about any possible poisoning.

After breakfast, Dr. Bowen decided to visit the Bordens. Although he didn't think anyone had been poisoned, he wanted to check on the family's health. He saw Mr. Borden lying on the sofa. Andrew told the doctor he didn't feel quite right but he didn't think he needed any medicine. Dr. Bowen did not see Abby or Lizzie during his visit.

Despite their illness, the Borden family managed to eat some lunch, which they shared with John Morse, Mr. Borden's brother-in-law. In the early evening, Lizzie went out to visit her friend Alice Russell. She told her how everyone in the family had been sick the night before except Bridget, and all of them except the maid had eaten bread from the bakery. That made Lizzie wonder if something in the bread had made them ill, but Alice doubted that. Many people probably bought the same bread, and no one had reported widespread sickness in the neighborhood.

Some of Mrs. Borden's fears may have spread to Lizzie, as she then told Alice that perhaps the family's milk had been poisoned. Alice asked, "Well, how do you get your milk; how could it be poisoned?" Lizzie explained how they set out an empty can at night, and then someone came to fill it. The milk came from the Bordens' Swansea farm. Alice asked what time the delivery usually came, and Lizzie said around four a.m. Alice said, "Well, it is light at four. I shouldn't think anybody would dare to come then and tamper with the cans for fear somebody would see them."[30] Lizzie agreed.

But then the conversation took an even darker turn. Lizzie said, "I feel afraid sometimes that father has got an enemy . . . he has so much trouble with his men that come to see him."[31] In his business dealings, Andrew was known to sometimes be rude.

In general, people described him as someone quick to offer his opinion on different topics but not willing to listen to what others had to say. And he had his reputation for being cheap. Lizzie also knew that her father could be rude to people—even his own wife. When Abby had left that morning to see Dr. Bowen, Andrew had shouted that he wouldn't pay for the visit if the doctor wanted to charge her for it. When the doctor later visited the Borden house, Mr. Borden was rude to him too.

Sitting with Alice, Lizzie described a scene she had recently overheard. A stranger came to the house to discuss renting some of Mr. Borden's property. He told the man, "I don't care to let my property for such business."[32] People have wondered if the stranger maybe wanted to sell alcohol. Andrew didn't drink and strongly opposed the use of alcohol. The stranger became combative and Andrew ordered him to leave. Lizzie then noted that the family barn had been broken into twice, and she told her friend about the burglary that had taken place the year before. She told Alice that she feared someone might burn down the house. Worrying about that made Lizzie "feel as if I wanted to sleep with my eyes half open—with one eye open half the time."[33]

Lizzie stayed with her friend for a few hours before returning home. After locking the doors, she went right to her room. She did not know that her uncle John Morse was there, spending the night, though she had heard him in the house earlier in the day. He and Mr. Borden had spent some time talking about the farmland Andrew owned in Swansea. He was looking for someone new to run at least some of it for him. Lizzie did not see her uncle in the morning, either, as he ate breakfast early with Mr. and Mrs. Borden before heading out on business.

A QUIET MORNING TURNS VIOLENT

FOR BRIDGET SULLIVAN, the morning of August 4 was like any other. She got up to build a fire in the stove and then began to prepare breakfast. Afterward, Mrs. Borden asked her to wash the windows inside and out. Abby then did a little dusting. With each doing their chores, Bridget did not see Abby alive again.

Lizzie came down for her breakfast around nine a.m., though she was still not feeling well and ate very little. She saw her father before he left to run his errands, then she began to iron her handkerchiefs. She took several breaks from the chore, spending some time reading and bringing some clean clothes upstairs.

Sometime between nine and ten a.m., Abby Borden received the nineteen whacks from a hatchet or ax that ended her life. From what she said afterward, Lizzie never heard or saw anyone enter the house, and she didn't see her stepmother's dead body lying on the floor upstairs. Then, around ten forty-five, Lizzie heard Bridget let her father in. Soon after, Lizzie explained to Mr. Borden about the note Abby had received, asking her to come visit a sick friend. Bridget overheard Lizzie explain this, and then she went to tell Bridget herself about it too. Lizzie did not know whether her stepmother had actually gone out, and if she had, whether she had returned. For her part, Bridget had not seen anyone bring the note to the door or seen or heard Mrs. Borden leaving the house.

While Mr. Borden read and rested in the sitting room, Lizzie spent part of the time outside. She went to the barn to look for fishing sinkers that she planned to use the next time she visited the Marion cottage. Returning to the house, she found her father's body where she had last seen him, only now she could see blood and knew something was wrong. She called out to Bridget, who came down the stairs and saw the same grisly sight.

Following Lizzie's orders, Bridget went to Dr. Bowen's house, then returned when she discovered he wasn't home. Now Adelaide Churchill was there, and she soon left to look for a doctor too. While she was out, Churchill told several people about the trouble at the Bordens'. As the word spread, a news dealer named John Cunningham called the police, along with two local newspapers. The first officer on the scene was George Allen. He asked a neighbor of the Bordens, Charles Sawyer, to stand guard at the side door to the house. Allen ran to headquarters to report the scene, then returned with another officer. By noon, at least a dozen people were at the house, including more police, several doctors, a reporter, and John Morse.

———◆———

INVESTIGATING THE CRIME SCENE

THE POLICE SOON discovered that nothing had been taken from the house or Andrew Borden's body, ruling out robbery as a motive. On one of his fingers, Mr. Borden wore a gold ring that Lizzie had given him years before. The room where he was killed was in order, indicating there had not been a struggle between him and his killer. The police also searched the house to see if the murderer might be hiding somewhere, then checked neighboring yards. The hunt turned up nothing.

Assistant Marshal John Fleet arrived at 92 Second Street around eleven forty-five and took over the investigation. He questioned Lizzie in her bedroom. The officer referred to Abby as her mother, and Lizzie was quick to correct him—Abby was not her mother, but her stepmother. Lizzie told Fleet that she hadn't seen anyone around the house, but she had heard her father talking with someone at the front door before nine, before he had left for his errands. Lizzie didn't see the man, but thought that he "spoke like an Englishman" and that he was there on business. Lizzie didn't hear anything that indicated he and her father were arguing. But prompted by Alice Russell, Lizzie told Fleet that another man had come to the door a few weeks before, and he had seemed mad with Mr. Borden. Still, when Fleet asked if she knew anyone who would want to kill her father, she replied, "I did not know that he had an enemy in the world."[34]

Lizzie explained to Fleet that she had been out in the barn for a time, then had come back inside to find her father's body. To another officer, she said she hadn't heard anything before discovering Mr. Borden. Yet later, she said she had heard a noise—a groan, she told one person, a scraping sound, she told another—before entering the sitting room.

Lizzie also said that John Morse had been at the house the night before and that morning, but he had left before nine. Fleet asked if she suspected her uncle of the crime and Lizzie said no, since he had not returned before she discovered her father's body. Fleet later questioned Morse and learned he had an alibi to explain where he was when the murder occurred. Later Fleet noted that he never saw Lizzie show any strong emotion or cry while he was with her.

After he finished questioning Lizzie, Fleet joined several other officers in the cellar. They had found two axes and two hatchets. They were covered in dust or perhaps ash from the coal that powered the furnace. Fleet later said they saw a spot on one of the blades "and thought it might be blood," but after looking at it, "thought that it was rust."[35] Later, Fleet found the head to another hatchet, which had been broken off its handle. Unlike the other tools, it was not covered in dust. But instead of taking the hatchet head for further examination, he replaced it where he had found it. Fleet then led a search of the entire house but didn't find anything that could have been the murder weapon or any other clues.

Another officer, William Medley, saw something else in the basement. He spotted a pail with water and some bloody towels. He asked Lizzie about it, when Dr. Bowen was with her. Without going into details, Bowen said there was an explanation for the blood. Women of childbearing age go through menstruation, a few days of bleeding every four weeks. At the time, women did not talk about such things in public with men. Medley did ask Lizzie how long the pail had been there and she said three or four days. Bridget, though, told Medley otherwise; she said she had not noticed the pail before that day, and if it had been there earlier, she would have seen it and washed the bloody towels.

Lizzie Borden grew up in what is sometimes called the Victorian era, named for Great Britain's Queen Victoria, who ruled from 1837 to 1901. The middle and upper classes in both Victoria's country and the United States had very specific ideas about right and wrong behavior. These attitudes helped define the era. Part of proper conduct for Victorians was not talking about sex or private matters. And men and women were expected to play very set roles. Men worked outside the home and controlled government. Women were supposed to become mothers and raise families. If their families had money, both men and women were expected to help the less fortunate, as Lizzie did at her church and with the various organizations she joined. Many people of Lizzie's social background found it hard to believe that any woman could commit the brutal murders carried out in the Borden home.

Medley then went out to the barn. Lizzie had said she went to its second floor to look for the sinkers she needed to fish.

Medley saw that a layer of dust covered the floor, but he didn't see any footprints, except the ones he had made.

As news of the murders spread, a number of friends and neighbors stopped by the Borden home. One of them was Charles Henry Wells, who taught Sunday school with Lizzie at Central Church. He saw medical examiner Dr. William Dolan measuring the cuts on Mr. Borden's body. Wells later wrote in his diary, "The appearance of [Borden's] face was like a mass of raw meat. So many blows had been reined [sic] upon his head that there was no semblance to a human face."[36] Examining Mrs. Borden's body, Dr. Dolan could tell that she had been murdered first. The blood from her body had already started to solidify, while Mr. Borden's body still oozed a warm liquid.

At some point during the day, someone carried Abby Borden's body downstairs and put it next to her husband's. Dr. Dolan cut into the dead bodies of Mr. and Mrs. Borden and removed their stomachs. He had heard the rumors of possible poisoning and wanted experts to study whatever food was in the murder victims' stomachs. Dolan also put samples of the family's milk into jars so it could be tested for poison.

One possible clue came later in the day from Dr. Benjamin Handy. He owned the cottage in Marion that Lizzie and her friends sometimes used and was a respected figure in town, so the police were apt to believe what he said. Handy told them that around ten thirty that morning, he had gone by the Borden house and seen a man in the area. The man caught the doctor's attention because he was walking very slowly and seemed very pale. Handy thought he might have seen the man in the neighborhood before, but he wasn't sure. Over the next few days, the police asked Handy to identify two men they thought fit the description of the man Handy saw. The doctor, though, did not recognize either one as the man he saw on the morning of August 4.

———◆———

IN THE EVENING

THE ACTIVITY AROUND the Borden house did not end as night fell. Local residents continued to crowd the street, hungry for details and passing along rumors. The *Fall River Herald* reported some of the stories that swirled around the city that first night and the next morning. One was that some carpenters saw a man on the morning of the fourth carrying "a cleaver entirely unlike anything they had ever seen." The cleaver was huge and rusty, and the man carrying it was poorly dressed. The carpenters were sure "that the cleaver they saw was the means by which Mr. Borden and his wife were killed."[37]

Yet the same news article said that people connected to the case agreed that "the murderer knew his ground and carried out his bloodthirsty plan with a speed and surety that indicated a well matured plot." The paper suggested that the earlier rumor of a Portuguese worker being a prime suspect was now "looked on with suspicion."[38] Whoever had committed the murders, not everyone in Fall River was upset on hearing the news of Andrew Borden's death. Some of the tenants in the commercial space he rented were tired of Borden often raising the rent. In some parts of Fall River, it was said that "someone had done a good job" when they killed him.[39]

By the evening, Emma Borden had returned home. The telegraph she had received from Dr. Bowen didn't give details about what was wrong; it merely said her father was sick. Emma saw the crowd in front of her house and knew something terrible had happened. She finally learned of her father's and stepmother's deaths when she reached 92 Second Street, and she was badly shaken by the news. The Borden sisters and Alice Russell spent the night at the house. In what must have been a bizarre and upsetting scene, the Bordens' hacked bodies were still in the house, waiting to undergo an autopsy the next day. To calm Lizzie's nerves, Dr. Bowen had given her some medication. Later he prescribed another drug for the same reason.

Outside the home, several police officers stood guard. One of them was Joseph Hyde. Around eight thirty, Russell came to tell him the three women were locking the doors and going to bed. A little later, looking through the cellar window, Hyde saw Lizzie and Russell enter the cellar, and Lizzie emptied something into the sink. It turned out to be a slop pail from upstairs. Then, about fifteen minutes later, the officer saw Lizzie return to the basement alone. Once again she went to the sink, but this time Hyde couldn't tell what she was doing. Then around ten p.m., the house went dark. But that night, the Fall River police were still working, and they found a witness who pointed the first finger of guilt at Lizzie Borden.

5

SUSPECT

Hearing the stories of possible poisoning in the Borden home, the police set out to question workers at local drugstores. Perhaps the murder suspect had tried to purchase a deadly chemical in the days before the murders. It didn't take long for Officers Doherty and Harrington to find a lead. Around six p.m., they visited a drugstore a few blocks from the Borden home. Working that night was Eli Bence. When the officers asked if anyone had recently tried to buy poison, Bence described an encounter he had had the day before. Around ten thirty a.m., a woman had come into the store and asked for a small amount of prussic acid. Known by scientists as hydrogen cyanide, this chemical can be created in the lab but also appears naturally in the pits and seeds of some fruit and in other plants. Some rat and insect poisons once contained prussic acid. People can survive a small dose of the chemical, but in large enough quantities it can be deadly. In ancient times the Romans used natural sources of prussic acid to poison their enemies.

Speaking to Harrington and Doherty, Bence said that the woman, whom he knew only as Miss Borden, told him she needed the prussic acid for a sealskin cape she owned. The chemical was sometimes used to kill moths that ate at clothing. Bence informed her that he could not sell the prussic acid without a doctor's prescription. She said she had bought some before without a prescription, but Bence was adamant, telling the customer, "Well, my good lady, it is a very dangerous thing to handle."[40] The woman then left the drugstore without buying anything.

Bence didn't realize the woman was Lizzie Borden until two other clerks in the store at the time later told him. The police asked him if he would recognize her if he saw her again or heard her voice. Bence said yes, and Harrington and Doherty took him to 92 Second Street. As Harrington talked to Lizzie, Bence stood in the back hallway and saw that she was the same person who had come asking for prussic acid the day before. As Bence later said, he had never had another customer come into the store seeking to buy prussic acid. For her part, Lizzie denied that she had tried to buy prussic acid from Bence.

A REAL POISONER AT WORK

Seven years before the Borden murders grabbed Americans' attention, another series of murders in Massachusetts made the news. Sarah Jane Robinson of Somerville was an Irish immigrant, and she and her husband, Moses, had trouble paying their bills. In 1881 Sarah Jane offered to take care of her sick landlord, but he ended up dying. Sarah Jane sent the family a bill for her nursing services. They agreed instead to forgive some of the family's rent. What no one could explain was what happened to $3,000 that went missing from the landlord's house.

Over the next few years, several relatives of Sarah Jane's

died, including her husband, her sister, and her sister's husband, and Sarah Jane collected on their life insurance. While taking care of her sister, Sarah Jane expressed the view that she would never recover, though the statement did not seem meaningful at the time. When Sarah Jane's own son was slowly dying, a suspicious doctor collected a sample of his vomit. When tested, it revealed traces of the poison arsenic. Sarah Jane was soon arrested and tried for murder. The poisoning led law enforcement officials to dig up the bodies of other people close to Sarah Jane who had died, including her sister. Their bodies contained arsenic too. Sarah Jane Robinson proclaimed her innocence, but a jury found her guilty of murder in 1888. She was sentenced to hang, but public opposition to executing a woman saved her life and her sentence was changed to life in jail.

The Robinson case came up again after the Borden murders, when some people tried to suggest that a woman couldn't carry out such a terrible crime. The Robinson case suggested that if Sarah Jane could kill her own relatives, perhaps Lizzie could too.

News of Bence's meeting with the police soon hit the newspapers. So did the announcement that Emma and Lizzie were offering a $5,000 reward for information that led to the arrest and conviction of their parents' killer. Already, though, some people in Fall River were talking about Lizzie being a possible suspect. Some also wondered if John Morse had played a part in the killings. Although a native of Massachusetts, Morse had spent most of his life in Iowa, where he made money buying and selling horses, among other business ventures. Horse traders like Morse were sometimes considered shady businessmen, as they tried to get the most money they could for their horses. Morse, though, was generally considered honest, but that didn't stop the police from carefully watching his movements.

On the night of the fifth, with hundreds of people still filling the street outside the Borden home, Morse slipped out of the house to mail a letter. The crowd, perhaps frustrated that the police didn't have any leads in the case, began to chase Morse. Before anyone could grab him and perhaps hurt him, the police assigned to tail him led him to safety. The next day Morse told reporters that "it was a terrible thing to be suspected and shadowed" as he had been, but he welcomed a thorough police investigation.[41]

On Saturday about seventy-five people came to the Borden house for a short memorial service for Andrew and Lizzie Borden, and then the mourners and the bodies headed to Oak Grove Cemetery. Several thousand people lined Second Street, hoping to see Lizzie for the first time since the murders. Several hundred more waited at the cemetery. The newspapers had widely differing views on how she acted that day. The *New York Times* reported that Lizzie's "nerves were completely unstrung, as was shown by the trembling of her body."[42] But the *Fall River Herald* said, "she walked with a firm and steady step to her seat in the carriage."[43] After a brief service at the cemetery, the Bordens' bodies were put in a storage vault. Dr. Dolan still hadn't performed an autopsy and wouldn't do so until the following week.

SEARCHING 92 SECOND STREET

WHILE THE FUNERAL was going on, the Fall River police once again searched the Borden home, as well as the barn and yard.

They were particularly interested in finding the murder weapon and perhaps bloody clothing that the killer might have worn. By now, Lizzie was becoming their prime suspect.

Dr. Dolan was there for the search, and he told a newspaper, "We examined everything, down to the slightest bump in the wallpaper."[44] As the search dragged on through the day, Lizzie returned to the house, along with her lawyer, Andrew Jennings. He turned over to police the dress Lizzie wore the day of the murders. The police also took the hatchets and axes they had left behind in the cellar.

That evening, Fall River mayor John Coughlin went to the Borden house with Marshal Rufus Hilliard, chief of the local police. They passed through the large crowd that still lingered on the sidewalk and in the street. The crowd was so thick that the two men in their horse-drawn carriage almost ran down some of the onlookers. Entering the house, the mayor and the police chief sat down with Emma, Lizzie, and John Morse. Coughlin said, "I have a request to make of the family, and that is that you remain in the house for a few days, as I believe it would be better for all concerned." Lizzie responded quickly, asking, "Why, is there anybody in this house suspected?"[45] Coughlin said that Morse's experience the night before with the mob should answer that question. People in Fall River were suspicious that someone in the household had committed the crime.

Lizzie pushed the mayor further, saying, "I want to know the truth." The mayor said, "Miss Borden, I regret to answer, but I must answer yes, you are suspected."[46] Lizzie then said that the police could take her away that moment, if they wished. Mayor Coughlin offered to have the police clear the people in the street, if the Bordens wanted, and assured them the police would protect them as they stayed in the house.

Reporting on the events of August 6, the *New York Herald* noted the growing suspicion about Lizzie, primarily because of her alleged attempt to buy poison. The paper, though, said she had no reason to kill her father and stepmother. If she were sane—and the paper had no reason to think she was insane—"it was inconceivable that she could have dispatched the old people, gone to the barn for the purpose of concealing the weapon . . . and then returned to play the part of a bereaved daughter so well."[47]

But at least one person who knew the Bordens thought

that Lizzie did have a motive. Hiram Harrington was married to Andrew Borden's sister Laurana. He described to a reporter his brother-in-law's stubborn nature when it came to money. To him, it was clear that whoever had committed the murders expected to gain financially. "If Mr. Borden died, he would have left something over $500,000, and all I will say is that, in my opinion, that furnishes the only motive." With that comment, Harrington made clear that he suspected a Borden family member, and Lizzie was the only one there at the time of the murder. But even as he suggested Lizzie could be the murderer, he said, "Right down in my heart I could not say I believed the party [Lizzie] guilty."[48]

<hr />

FEELINGS FOR AND AGAINST LIZZIE

ON SUNDAY, AUGUST 7, Dr. Dolan and John Fleet of the Fall River police force took one of the hatchets found in the Borden cellar to the cemetery. Going to the vault that held the dead bodies of

Andrew and Abby Borden, they tried to see if the shape of the blade matched the wounds the couple had received. The two men could not tell for sure if the hatchet was the murder weapon.

That day, people who attended Central Congregational Church heard the minister talk about the murders. Reverend W. Walker Jubb warned people not to give in to the rumors being spread and unfairly accuse someone of the crime. The murderer, he was convinced, "must have been without heart, without soul, a fiend incarnate, the very vilest of degraded and depraved humanity, or he must have been a maniac." He also called on the local press not to report rumors, and while he did not mention Lizzie by name, Jubb seemed to know that she faced growing suspicion. He called on the congregation not to "blacken and blast" the reputation of someone who "has always commanded respect, whose acts and motives have always been pure and holy."[49]

Still, some people in town were ready to see Lizzie as the guilty party. The incident at the drugstore was widely known, and some people talked about the strained relationship between Lizzie and her stepmother. That belief seemed reinforced on Monday, August 8, when Officer William Medley talked with

Augusta Tripp. She and Lizzie had been friends for years, and Lizzie had sometimes visited her in Westport, Massachusetts, where Tripp lived then. Tripp recounted how Lizzie told her "she thought her stepmother was deceitful, being one thing to her face and another to her back."[50] Lizzie also thought that Abby had influence over her father. As evidence, she brought up the incident from five years before, when Mr. Borden had paid for half of Abby's stepmother's house. Money was on Lizzie's mind again when she told Tripp, "I do not know that my sister and I would get anything in the event of my father's death."[51]

Tripp gave her statement just one day before the first legal proceeding in the Borden murders. Under Massachusetts law, a judge conducted an inquest whenever a mysterious death occurred. The goal was to see if the state could present enough evidence to show that someone should be arrested for the crime. Lizzie Borden would have another chance to describe what she saw and did on the morning her parents were hacked to death.

6

LIZZIE SPEAKS

Lizzie Borden had answered questions all day on August 4, as first one officer and then another tried to discover the facts surrounding the murder of Mr. and Mrs. Borden. On Tuesday, August 9, she would answer questions posed by Hosea Knowlton, the district attorney for southern Massachusetts. In that position, his job was to prosecute and try to convict people charged with a crime. At the inquest, he would question many of the people who had been at the Borden home on August 4.

The day before the inquest, Knowlton met with Rufus Hilliard, chief of the Fall River police, several other officers, and Dr. Dolan. Hilliard felt some pressure from parts of the community to make an arrest, and he and his men strongly considered Lizzie a suspect. But they also knew her position in Fall River's powerful Yankee ruling class. Her family had money, and she was respected for her church work. The *Fall River Herald* reported that Lizzie's friends had tried to contradict some of the public statements that described her as cold and without emotion. The friends talked about her "womanly characteristics," which suggested a woman of her background could not possibly be a ruthless killer.[52]

Ethnic divisions in Fall River were also in the background of the investigation. The city's mayor and many of the police officials were Irish—a sign of that ethnic group's growing influence in Fall River. Their gains came at a time when some New England Yankees—including at least one Fall River minister—were speaking out against the arrival of even more immigrants who were not Protestant like they were. One newspaper read primarily by the city's Irish, the *Fall River Daily Globe*, voiced its suspicions that Lizzie was the killer, and unlike many other papers, backed the police efforts against her.

Some modern observers have seen those anti-immigrant feelings in Lizzie, too. Neither she nor her sister called Bridget Sullivan by her actual name. Instead they called her Maggie—the name of the previous Irish housekeeper who had worked for the Bordens. It seemed to some that the Borden sisters couldn't even be bothered to learn Bridget's name, or that they thought one Irish servant was just like another. Then, on the day of the murder, when Lizzie learned from Bridget that Dr. Bowen was not home, she didn't send the servant to see if either of the other two doctors who lived on Second Street were home. One was Irish, one was French Canadian, and both were Roman Catholic.

If Lizzie did share the prejudices of many Yankees of the era, she at least didn't try to focus attention on Bridget as a suspect, as some city residents did. When questioned by police, Lizzie said that Bridget had been outside washing windows when the murders occurred. Along with having an alibi, Bridget didn't have a motive for the murder. She didn't stand to gain any money from the Bordens' death, and she had good relations with the parents. (They, unlike their daughters, at least called Bridget by her real name.)

THE INQUEST

IN HIS MEETING with Hilliard and the others, Knowlton went over all the information the police had gathered so far. Hilliard presented him with a stack of police reports that was three feet high. From these the officers gathered the most important pages and spread them out for Knowlton and his assistants to review. According to the *Herald*, several facts posed problems. Lizzie had said she had gone to the upper floor, or loft, of the barn to get fishing sinkers. Yet the police didn't see any footprints in the dust that had settled on the floor, except their own. Had the shock of the murders led her to misspeak? Or was it a lie?

Then Knowlton considered the note Abby Borden supposedly got on August 4, asking her to go visit a sick friend. Lizzie said her stepmother told her about the note, but no one in the house had seen it. And since the murder, no one had stepped forward to say he or she had written such a note, and no one admitted delivering it. Even after public pleas for information about the note, the police had no details on it. Lizzie had said that perhaps her stepmother had burned it in the kitchen stove.

NOT ALL EVIDENCE IS THE SAME

As Hosea Knowlton went over the information the police had gathered, he must have seen what others had: the evidence that suggested Lizzie Borden might be a murderer was circumstantial. This kind of evidence relies on examining facts and drawing conclusions from them. For instance, a person who could not look out the window to see the weather might be able to realistically conclude it's raining if she sees several people come in from outside with wet umbrellas. The other kind of evidence is direct. The person could tell it's raining by going outside and feel the water hitting her body. Direct evidence also includes physical items connected to a crime, such as a hair or piece of clothing the criminal left behind. Circumstantial evidence can be used to convict someone of a crime. But a defense lawyer might be able to show that the conclusions drawn from such evidence are not necessarily the only possible conclusions. In this way, defense lawyers try to make a jury doubt an alleged criminal's guilt.

Knowlton's meeting with the officers dragged on late into the night of August 8. The next day he went to the courtroom above the police station for the inquest. The judge in charge of it was Josiah Blaisdell. He had once served as mayor of Fall River and had been a judge for almost twenty years. Together, he and Knowlton denied Lizzie's lawyer's request to represent her at the inquest. The lawyer, Andrew Jennings, argued that Lizzie had already been named a suspect by the mayor, even if she hadn't been arrested. The inquest was a legal proceeding and she would be under oath, but Blaisdell and Knowlton didn't believe the law required them to let Lizzie have her lawyer there. At that point, since she was a suspect, Lizzie could have refused to speak at the inquest. But she and Jennings decided that if she didn't testify, she would stoke the feelings some residents already had about her guilt.

As word spread that Lizzie was leaving her house to go to the inquest, hundreds of people across Fall River stopped what they were doing and tried to get a look at her. They filled the streets as her carriage rolled toward the police station. The carriage had a black curtain covering its windows that kept the onlookers from seeing her. Edwin Porter, who covered the Borden murders for the *Fall River Daily Globe*, later wrote a book about the case called *The Fall River Tragedy*. He described the scene on the morning of August 9: "Windows were thrown open, heads were thrust out, crowds pushed through the streets and for ten minutes it seemed as if the whole town within a stone's throw of police headquarters was vibrating. . . . The community had reached a point when it felt that it must clear up the mystery, or go insane."[53]

In the courtroom, Knowlton, Blaisdell, Mayor Coughlin, and several police officials waited for Borden and the other witnesses called to testify. Among them were Bridget Sullivan; John Morse; Abby Borden's half sister, Sarah Whitehead; and Lizzie's friend Augusta Tripp. Some of the testimony from the three-day inquest has been lost, and no reporters were allowed into the courtroom. Each witness appeared alone, so they couldn't hear what the others said.

Bridget Sullivan testified first, and the *Fall River Herald* commented, "If an honest appearing face was to acquit a person of a crime Miss Sullivan has that face." The paper also reported that some people in Fall River believed that if the person suspected of the murders were poor, "they would have been locked up long before now."[54] The police denied this, but the notion reflected the feeling some later held that Lizzie was given special treatment because of her privileged background.

LIZZIE'S TESTIMONY

LIZZIE SPOKE THAT afternoon and would face questioning two more times during the three-day inquest. The record of her testimony does survive, and students of the case see the same thing Hosea Knowlton did. Lizzie told differing accounts of what happened on the day of the murder and during the inquest. Unlike on the fourth, she did not mind when Knowlton referred to Mrs. Borden as her mother. She tried to paint a picture of having a good relationship with Abby, if not a close, loving one. She said the only time she "had words" with Abby was over her half sister's house. Lizzie added, "They were not hard words. It was simply a difference of opinion."[55]

Knowlton pressed Lizzie on her relationship with Abby, drawing out that Lizzie began calling her stepmother Mrs. Borden after the house incident. Yet Lizzie insisted that in some ways, their relationship was like a mother and a daughter, though she declined to say how, "because I don't know how to answer."[56] She would say something like that several times as she seemed to try to avoid answering some of Knowlton's questions. Other times she seemed bothered by the questioning, especially as she struggled to remember the events. She seemed unsure about where she had been when her father returned home on August 4. First she said she was not upstairs, and then she said she was. She denied some of the things she had told the police, Bridget, and Adelaide Churchill that day. Lizzie had said to Bridget that she heard Abby return from visiting a friend, yet at the inquest she denied it. At one point she said, "I have answered so many questions and I am so confused I don't know one thing from another."[57]

On her second day of testimony, Lizzie again contradicted

some of what she had said before. On Tuesday she said she had spent some time upstairs after her father left in the morning. Now she said she had not gone up after he left. She also changed her story about how long she was out in the barn after her father returned home, saying it was only fifteen or twenty minutes. She had told the police on the fourth that it was longer. But even with the shorter stay, Knowlton said that finding the fishing sinkers should have taken only a few minutes. Lizzie now said that she had taken some pears from a tree in the backyard and eaten several of them, both before and while she was in the barn.

This explanation seemed to puzzle Knowlton, as Lizzie had earlier said she did not feel well enough to eat breakfast that morning, after the slight case of food poisoning she experienced on Wednesday the third. The loft of the barn was particularly hot, and Knowlton couldn't imagine why she would leisurely stay up there and eat pears, especially if she had not been feeling so well just several hours before. At one point, Knowlton grew frustrated as Lizzie would not answer his questions directly. "You did not answer my question and you will, if I have to put it all day." He then tried to learn why she'd picked that spot, where she could not clearly see the house, at that time, to eat pears. "I cannot tell you any reason," Lizzie replied.[58]

Knowlton also prodded Lizzie about the various axes and hatchets in the basement. She said she knew there was one old ax in the cellar, but she didn't know anything about a hatchet. The prosecutor asked if she knew anything about blood on the ax, or if anyone had killed any animals at the home. Lizzie said no, but she did describe an incident that is still often recounted when people discuss the case. She said her father had killed several pigeons a few months before, and that she assumed Andrew had wrung their necks. Her father then brought the dead pigeons into the house, some with their heads on, some with them off. The missing heads, she said, did not seem to have been cut off.

On the last day of the inquest, Lizzie denied that she had gone to the drugstore to buy prussic acid, though Eli Bence and one of his coworkers testified under oath that she had. Lizzie said she didn't even know where the drugstore was, though it was located not far from her house. As Lizzie's testimony came to a close, Knowlton asked if she knew anything else that might be a useful clue in tracking down her parents' killer. Lizzie said that about two weeks before the murder, she saw a man by the side door of the house. She had never told this to any of the officers, only her lawyer.

ARRESTED

THAT AFTERNOON, AUGUST 11, the inquest ended. Knowlton met with Marshal Hilliard and told him to issue a warrant for Lizzie's arrest. Apparently he had heard enough during the three days of testimony to question her story and her innocence. While the police were still following up leads to see if someone outside the family had killed Andrew and Abby Borden, Knowlton was now focusing on Lizzie.

That evening Lizzie was with Emma and a friend in a room in the police station when Andrew Jennings informed her she was about to be arrested. Knowlton and Hilliard showed up to read the warrant, which spelled out the crime she was charged with. Jennings said there was no need for them to read it. Using the stiff language of the law, the warrant said that Lizzie had killed her father with a hatchet with "malice aforethought."[59] That meant she had planned the murder in advance and meant to kill him. The warrant did not mention the murder of Abby Borden.

As with much of the case, reporters could not agree on what happened next. The *New York Times* said, "The lady took the announcement of her arrest with surprising calmness." But the *New York Herald* reported that "a fit of violent trembling seized her."[60] Lizzie spent the night at the police station, while Emma went home in tears. Instead of staying in a cell, Lizzie was allowed to sleep in the bedroom reserved for the matron, the woman who looked after female prisoners.

The next day, despite some rain, hundreds of Fall River residents once again flocked to the police station. News had spread of Lizzie's arrest, and now some people hoped to see her arraignment. During his legal procedure, a judge reads the charges against the defendant—the person accused of a crime. The defendant then responds to the charges by pleading guilty or not guilty. In this case, Andrew Jennings waived the reading of the complaint against Lizzie. He wanted to enter her plea for her, but District Attorney Knowlton insisted she give it herself.

Lizzie had been calm since entering the court, but now she said, "Not guilty" in a quiet voice. The court's clerk asked her to repeat it. This time, the *New York Times* reported, "she raised her voice and said in quite a loud tone, 'Not guilty!' putting strong emphasis on the first word."[61]

Murder was a capital offense in Massachusetts, meaning Lizzie could be executed if she were found guilty. Since this was a capital case, the judge decided not to set bail—money that lets an accused criminal be released after they are arraigned. Lizzie left the courtroom and was soon on a train to Taunton, Massachusetts. She would stay in a jail there until the next legal proceeding took place—a preliminary hearing. Now her lawyer would hear the evidence against her and be able to plan his defense.

After the arraignment, a reporter from the *Fall River Herald* interviewed Marshal Hilliard and two other top officers investigating the case. The reporter wrote that the men were sure they had the evidence that could "establish the theory we adopted at the start. . . .When the case is publicly heard people will be satisfied with the evidence we shall offer, and so will the jury."[62] The officers, however, were not going to tip their hand about the evidence they had. One fact was known by then, however: the Borden family's milk had not been poisoned, as Lizzie had suggested it might have been. Meanwhile, the police continued to search for more clues, following up on various rumors. And Lizzie would soon be in a cell, waiting to see what would happen next.

7

THE PRELIMINARY HEARING

Leaving the arraignment, Lizzie rode in a carriage with Marshal Hilliard, a detective, and Reverend Edwin Buck, one of the ministers from Central Congregational Church. One reporter wrote, "To all outward appearances, she was as calm as though she had been going for a visit to relatives."[63] Police held back the crowd that was waiting for them at the train station, as many people in Fall River remained eager to try to catch a glimpse of the city's most famous accused criminal. By one account, Lizzie seemed to slump a bit as she walked and relied on Reverend Buck and Hilliard for support.

On the train ride, Lizzie kept her eyes down and didn't say a word. When the train pulled into Taunton, another crowd met it. The residents there were just as eager to see the alleged murderer. When Lizzie reached the Bristol County Jail, she saw two familiar faces. Sheriff Andrew Wright and his wife, Mary Jane, had once lived in Fall River. They had been friends with Andrew Borden, and Lizzie and their daughter Isabel had sometimes played together. Mrs. Wright cried when she saw Lizzie, and her husband fought back his own tears.

Despite her friendship with the Wrights, Lizzie at first was treated just like any other prisoner. She had to take a bath, then she was led into a cell that measured nine and a half feet by seven and a half feet. Over time, though, Lizzie received one benefit the other prisoners didn't: the Wrights arranged for a nearby hotel restaurant to prepare some of her meals. While in jail, Lizzie spent her time reading, thought she didn't ask for the daily newspapers—perhaps because she didn't want to read what they were reporting about her case.

In the days before the preliminary hearing, papers across the country began to take a strong stand about Lizzie's innocence or guilt. The *Fall River Daily Globe* reported that most New England papers "were sneering at the police," believing they had botched the investigation.[64] Those papers, the *Globe* said, also supported Lizzie's innocence. The *Globe* itself, with its largely Irish-Catholic readership, took the other view.

Its competitor, the *Fall River Herald*, was one of the newspapers that backed Lizzie. It used a phrase that soon spread to other papers, calling the legal proceedings a "star chamber" against Lizzie. That phrase referred to a special court that had existed in England until the seventeenth century. The Star Chamber operated outside of the legal rules used in other English courts and did not have a jury. Instead judges and some of the king's councillors decided cases. During the 1620s and 1630s, King Charles I used the Star Chamber to promote his own power over Parliament, which led that lawmaking body to end it. To Lizzie's supporters, the legal process being used against her seemed unfair and an abuse of power—as many English had come to see their country's Star Chamber.

Reporting on Lizzie's arrival in Taunton, the *Herald* quoted Reverend Buck's comments after spending time with Lizzie in the jail. He said, "Her calmness is the calmness of innocence." The paper went on to call Lizzie "a remarkable woman" who lacked the "weaknesses of her sex" that most women usually showed.[65]

Speculation about what would happen at the preliminary hearing went on for ten days, as Lizzie sat in her cell. At one point, a man named Charles Peckham went to the Fall River police and said he had committed the murders. As the *New York Times* reported, Peckham said he killed the couple "out of pure love for blood" and demanded to be locked up.[66] The police soon discovered that Peckham had had mental health issues for some time and released him.

The police also received tips and letters from people claiming to know something about the murders—or even confessing to them. A man named Joseph Lemay said he saw a man holding a bloody ax during the time while Lizzie was in Taunton. Lemay said he approached the man and spoke to him in French, and the man ran off into the woods. The police searched the woods but didn't discover anything. The police also received a letter from someone who called himself or herself "See Me Not." He said he had killed Andrew Borden because "I was in jail . . . on old Borden's account, and I meant to get even."[67]

───◆───

BACK TO FALL RIVER

AS THE PRELIMINARY hearing drew closer, Andrew Jennings was hard at work, trying to prepare Lizzie's defense. He issued a summons that directed Marshal Hilliard and Dr. Dolan to turn over all the evidence they had gathered. That included, the *Fall River Herald* reported, "the stomachs of the murdered persons" and "the pieces of carpet on which the blood from their wounds flowed."[68] Jennings refused to tell the newspapers why he requested what he did, who he would call as witnesses, or what information he and his assistant, Arthur Phillips, had gathered. He also instructed Emma Borden and John Morse not to speak to reporters.

Arthur Phillips had just graduated from law school when he began helping Andrew Jennings defend Lizzie Borden. Through the preliminary hearings and into the next year, Phillips did research and questioned potential witnesses. In 1894 he left Jennings's office and began working on his own. He died in 1941, but before his death he wrote a three-volume history of Fall River, which was published in 1946. In the third book, Phillips shared his memories and opinions of the Lizzie Borden case. Like all the lawyers who defended Lizzie, Phillips was convinced that she was innocent. Several Borden scholars have noted that Phillips made some factual errors when describing the case, which led some to think he did not write the section on Lizzie. For a time some people thought that the man who edited the third volume of Phillips's history actually wrote this section, using Phillips's notes. But today the scholars seem to agree that Phillips did write it.

The section of his book dealing with the Borden murders is now available online, thanks to Borden expert Stefani

Koorey. In her foreword to the online edition, Koorey wrote that Phillips's work gives a "rare glimpse . . . into the workings of Lizzie's defense and the arguments that they developed" to defend her in court.[69] Phillips ended his section on the trial by writing, "Others had far more reason to kill [Andrew Borden]" than Lizzie did.[70]

If Jennings would not say much to reporters, one of Lizzie's friends was eager to publicly defend her. Mary Ella Brigham had known Lizzie since the Borden family had lived on Ferry Street. She had also been with Lizzie after the last session of the inquest, when the police told Lizzie she was going to be arrested. Now, as the hearing approached, Brigham said that the stories of Lizzie not getting along with her stepmother and refusing to dine with both her parents were not true. "She has told me many times that these latter years have been her happiest." Brigham also dismissed any notion that Lizzie was insane, even for the brief time it might have taken to kill her parents. Then she recounted something Lizzie had worried about before. The house on 92 Second Street had an unusual layout, with the upstairs rooms connected and two sets of stairs. Lizzie, Brigham claimed, had said that "anyone might come in and go all over the house without anyone knowing it."[71]

On August 22 Lizzie traveled back to Fall River for the preliminary hearing. She managed to leave the Taunton jail without drawing a crowd, but some people waited outside the Fall River police station when she arrived there. Inside, spectators jammed the courtroom. As at the inquest, Judge Blaisdell was in charge of the proceedings. Prosecutor Hosea Knowlton didn't have to prove Lizzie was guilty, but he had to convince the judge that the state had enough evidence to show that she could have murdered her parents. For his part, as he reminded reporters, Jennings didn't have to prove that Lizzie was innocent. In the US court system, the defendant is assumed to be innocent until the prosecution proves otherwise.

The people who gathered in the court that day were disappointed when the judge granted Knowlton's request to delay the hearing. He was still waiting to hear back from the expert who was examining some of the evidence the police had collected, including the possible murder weapons found in the Bordens' cellar. Judge Blaisdell postponed the hearing until August 25.

Instead of returning to Taunton, Lizzie again stayed in the matron's room at the police station. Her uncle John brought her home-cooked meals prepared by Emma, and Reverend Buck brought her at least one book to read. On August 24 Emma came by for a visit. Hannah Reagan, the matron of the Fall River jail, heard part of a conversation between the two sisters. That afternoon Reagan repeated what she said she had heard to Edwin Porter of the *Fall River Daily Globe*. According to Reagan, when Emma walked into the room, Lizzie said, "You gave me away, Emma, didn't you?" Emma replied, "I only told Mr. Jennings what I thought he ought to know." This response, Reagan said, upset Lizzie, who said, "Remember, Emma, that I will never give in one inch, never."[72]

Reagan's report ended up in the local papers, and soon the matron found forces friendly to Lizzie questioning the story. Jennings and Reverend Buck told her to say the newspaper report was not true. Feeling pressured by these prominent people, Reagan did as they asked. Jennings wrote a statement for Reagan to sign. It read in part, "I expressly and positively deny that any such conversation ever took place and that I further deny that that I ever heard anything that could be construed as a quarrel between the two sisters."[73] Reagan, though, didn't want to sign the statement before showing it to Marshal Hilliard. He told her not to sign it and not to discuss what did or didn't happen the morning of the twenty-fourth unless she was called to testify in court. Reagan did not sign, and Jennings blamed Hilliard for interfering in the matter.

———◆———

THE HEARING BEGINS

ON AUGUST 25, several hours before the hearing would begin, people already began to crowd around the doorway of the court, hoping to get inside. Most of them were, as the *Fall River Herald* reported, "tastefully dressed women and respectable citizens of leisure," meaning people with money who did not have to work.[74] Few of Fall River's mill workers and maids could take a day off to witness the event.

A few minutes before ten a.m., the crowd in the courtroom began to whisper as Lizzie prepared to enter the room. Emma came ahead of her, holding the arm of a family friend, and then Lizzie came in with Reverend Buck. They watched as Knowlton began to question the witnesses the prosecutor hoped would convince Judge Blaisdell that Lizzie should be tried for murder.

One of the first witnesses was Dr. Dolan, the medical examiner. He described the two murder scenes as he found them on August 4, giving details of the wounds he saw on Andrew and Abby. He testified that he examined the hatchets the officers found and saw spots that might have been blood, but he wasn't sure. Dolan also described the blood spots and spatters he found in the house. Under questioning from Melvin Adams, one of Lizzie's two defense lawyers, Dolan publicly disclosed for the first time that he had cut off the heads of the two murder victims at the autopsy, before their bodies were buried. Massachusetts attorney general Albert Pillsbury had ordered him to so because Pillsbury wanted the skulls as evidence. Dolan cleaned the skulls and kept them in his office.

That news caused a stir in the courtroom, and people looked

to see how the Borden sisters reacted to hearing that their parents' bodies had been buried without their heads. Emma's eyes filled with tears, while Lizzie looked startled. Then she turned to look at her sister. But as the *Fall River Herald* noted, Lizzie's eyes had been "sharp and piercing" all morning, and "the shocking announcement did not dim their brilliancy."[75]

The other witnesses over the next week included Bridget Sullivan, Alice Russell, and Adelaide Churchill. On Monday afternoon, August 29, the audience gathered in the courtroom was eager to hear Eli Bence's testimony. His story of refusing to sell Lizzie some prussic acid was well known, but the crowd wanted to hear him tell his version of the events. When it was Melvin Adams's turn to question Bence, he tried to call into question the clerk's memory for detail, suggesting that perhaps it wasn't Lizzie he saw that day in the drugstore. Or perhaps when he went to the Borden house with the police on August 4, he might have misidentified Lizzie as the woman from the store. At one point Adams asked, "I suppose you are reasonably sure of the people you see, are you not?" Bence said yes, and Adams asked, "You never made any mistake did you?"

Bence replied, "Well, I don't suppose that there is anybody that never made a mistake."[76] Adams continued to hammer away at this, asking if Bence could have ever made a mistake about someone's identity. Bence insisted he never had.

<hr />

THE EXPERT

ONE OF THE key witnesses for the state was Professor Edward S. Wood of Harvard University. He was a doctor as well as an expert in chemistry. Wood had received the jars of milk and the victims' stomachs, which Dr. Dolan had prepared on August 4. Dolan also sent him the weapons found at the Borden house, along with clothing that Lizzie had worn the day of the killings.

At the hearing, Wood discussed what he had found in the Bordens' stomachs. He saw partially digested food that included bread, meat, and vegetables. He did not find any traces of prussic acid, though he had not tested for any other poisons. On the hatchets, Wood saw spots that to the naked eye looked like blood, but his tests showed it was not. Some hair found on one of the blades came from an animal, not a human. Of the possible bloodstains found on the clothing, only one small spot was actually blood. Under questioning by Adams, Wood said that the blows delivered to the Bordens' heads would most likely have left blood everywhere—certainly on a good part of the killer's clothes.

After that day, Lizzie's supporters felt better about her chances of being released. As the *Fall River Herald* said, everyone heard "blow after blow delivered to the government's theory, shattering it piece for piece. . . ."[77] Since Lizzie didn't have to testify at the hearing, Knowlton didn't get a second chance to question her. But he did read her responses from the inquest, which showed how she sometimes contradicted herself.

On August 31 the defense had a chance to call witnesses. Lizzie's lawyers wanted to show that the government had not proven its case against her. There was a strong possibility that an unknown person had been able to enter the Borden house undetected and commit the murders. The state had not found a murder weapon or any of Lizzie's clothing with blood on it. Speaking afterward to the *New York Times*, Adams said, "What has become of that [murder] weapon if Lizzie Borden is guilty?

Did it vanish into mid-air? No. The natural presumption must be that the murderer carried the instrument away with him."[78]

One key witness for the defense was Phebe Bowen, the wife of Dr. Seabury Bowen. She testified that on Wednesday, August 3, she saw Lizzie leave the Borden house around six p.m. Mrs. Bowen then went over to talk to Andrew and Abby, as she knew the family had been sick. According to Bowen, Abby told her that Lizzie was feeling better. "She has not been out all day, but she has gone now to see Alice Russell."[79] If this were true, then Lizzie did not leave the house to go to the drugstore, as Eli Bence had claimed.

The hearing ended on September 1, with each side presenting its closing argument. Jennings went first, noting that he had been friends with Andrew Borden, so this was not just any murder case to him. He then referred to Lizzie as a "girl" and brought up the idea again that the legal proceedings against her were a star chamber. He suggested that any contradictions in her statements to the police and at the inquest were not surprising, given how the authorities had virtually kept her a prisoner in her home after the fourth. Summing up his argument against the state's case, Jennings said, "They haven't proved that this girl had anything to do with the murder."[80] When Jennings finished, the courtroom erupted with applause, and some of Lizzie's supporters began to cry.

Knowlton closed out the proceedings by trying to show that Lizzie had a motive for the killings, though at this point she was only being charged with her father's murder. He pointed out how Lizzie had stopped referring to Abby as her mother and asserted that "no more lasting hatred ever springs up than between step-parents and their children."[81] He also mentioned the quarrel between the sisters and their stepmother over the house on Fourth Street.

Knowlton talked about the house being locked up on the day of the murder and wondered how, on a fairly busy street, no one had seen anyone enter or leave the house. Then he stressed Lizzie's response to the murders: "While everybody is dazed there is but one person who, throughout the whole business, has not been seen to express emotion." He went on, "This was not a crime of a moment. It was conceived in the head of a cunning, cool woman."[82]

Around three forty-five that afternoon, Judge Blaisdell announced his decision. He said he would prefer it if he could say, "Lizzie, I judge you probably not guilty. You may go home." And he thought that he would win popular support if he said that. But if Knowlton had presented the same evidence against a man, even if it were circumstantial, everyone would have expected him to agree with the state that the legal proceedings should go on. "So," Blaisdell continued, "there is only one thing to do, painful as it may be—the judgment of the Court is that you are probably guilty."[83]

The reporters who covered the trial did not record how Lizzie reacted to Judge Blaisdell's announcement of her probable guilt. But when she returned to her room in the police station, she gave "a single outbreak of grief," the *Herald* said, as she considered spending more time as a prisoner.[84] The next morning she would go back to the jail in Taunton to await the next step in her legal battle.

8

FACING THE GRAND JURY

A familiar scene played out on the afternoon of September 2. A crowd of people waited around the Fall River police station, hoping to see Lizzie as she made another trip to Taunton. Just before one p.m., the onlookers saw Lizzie leave the station with Reverend Buck. Lizzie would be held at the Bristol County Jail until a grand jury met in November. The grand jury would hear evidence and decide if the state had a strong enough case against Lizzie to put her on trial for murder.

Reverend Buck, who had spent so much time with Lizzie after the murders, remained convinced of her innocence. So did her closest friends, and while Lizzie stayed in her cell, many came to visit her. They included Elizabeth Johnston, who belonged to Lizzie's church and was part of the group of young ladies who sometimes stayed at the cottage in Marion. Johnston brought Lizzie books and magazines and sometimes stayed with her in her cell throughout the day.

Lizzie also stayed connected to friends by writing letters. One that survives today went to Annie Lindsey. The two women had been friends since childhood, and Lizzie wrote her several times while she was in jail. In October, Lizzie wrote about Daisy, the jailhouse cat, and told Annie not to send her a teakettle, as she had no place to store it. Then Lizzie wrote about her situation: "Why do you tell me to keep up my courage a *little* while longer? *My* counsel [lawyers] gives me no hopes of anything *soon*, or ever of an *acquittal*. Your dreams are too rosy, for they must know."[85]

Along with reading, writing letters, and visiting with guests, Lizzie sometimes walked through the prison for exercise. Mrs. Wright, the sheriff's wife, let her tend several window boxes filled with flowers. While she enjoyed privileges that other prisoners didn't, Lizzie still grappled with the knowledge that she didn't know how long she would be locked up. As her letter to Annie Lindsey showed, she knew she could be found guilty.

———◆———

SEVERAL MONTHS OF WAITING

WITH LIZZIE'S RETURN to the Taunton jail, she won new support from different people and organizations across the country. Susan Fessenden, the president of the Massachusetts chapter of the Woman's Christian Temperance Union (WCTU), spoke out for her. She asked Massachusetts governor William E. Russell to arrange for Lizzie to be granted bail, noting Lizzie's "30 years of virtuous living."[86] Members of the WCTU from across the country wrote to Lizzie, trying to boost her spirits.

Another defender was Mary Livermore, who was active in the movement to give women the right to vote. Livermore had once lived in Fall River and been friendly with Lizzie's mother, Sarah. Livermore met with Lizzie in jail and then spoke to major newspapers, declaring her belief in Lizzie's innocence. She told the *New York Times*, "It has been my opinion from the first that it [the crime] was the work of a maniac."[87] Livermore then said that she didn't think it was difficult to believe that someone could have entered and left the house without being seen. She had gone in and out of her own house at times with no one inside noticing her.

MARY LIVERMORE AND THE SUFFRAGISTS

While many women of the Victorian Age accepted their unequal position in society compared to men, Mary Livermore was one who did not. She became active in political issues during the 1840s, speaking out against slavery and calling for it to be abolished. After the Civil War, she became a leader of the suffragist movement in the United States, an effort to give all American women the right to vote. By the time of the Lizzie Borden trial, some states and US territories had given women the right to vote in local elections. But Massachusetts, among others, had not, and no women in the country could vote for president. While Livermore had a personal connection to Lizzie, other suffragists also spoke in defense of Lizzie. The suffragists, as Joseph A. Conforti argues in his *Lizzie Borden on Trial,* "saw respectable native-born women like Lizzie as precisely the types who needed to be empowered with the right to vote and to serve on juries."[88] Given the laws of the time, all the members of the two juries who weighed the evidence against her were men.

While Lizzie had her supporters, news sometimes came out that put her in a bad light. One report in the *Fall River Herald* said that before one of her visits with her friend to the cottage in Marion, Massachusetts, Lizzie volunteered for the chore of chopping wood. When she was told the ax at the cottage was dull, she supposedly said not to worry—she had a sharp one she could bring along.

During her time back in jail, Lizzie gave several interviews while waiting for the grand jury. Andrew Jennings arranged for reporters who supported her to come to the jail. One of them was Kate Swan McGuirk, who wrote for several publications.

She had once lived in Fall River and knew the accused murderer. Lizzie told her, "I know I am innocent, and I have made up my mind that no matter what happens, I will try to bear it bravely and make the best of it."[89]

While Lizzie sat in jail, the Fall River police were still trying to uncover more evidence against her. Marshal Hilliard hired a private detective out of Providence, Rhode Island, named Edward McHenry. He didn't seem to provide useful evidence, but he did manage to earn extra money by spreading lies about the case. He told a reporter from the *Boston Globe* that for $500, he would reveal details about the Borden family and the murders that only the police knew. The reporter, a young man named Henry Trickey, was eager to beat out rival papers for this news and so paid the bribe. Most of what McHenry told him, however, was untrue. Neither Trickey nor the *Globe* tried to verify the information, and so the public soon read a long front-page story filled with lies about the case. Lizzie and her supporters heard of the false story too, and they burned with anger over it.

Trickey's story said that the prosecution had found several witnesses who had heard Lizzie arguing with her father the night before the murders. The witnesses all said they heard the two discussing Lizzie's relations with an unnamed man, who had supposedly gotten her pregnant. Another part of the story said that several witnesses claimed to have seen Lizzie and Abby in the upstairs room where Abby was killed. They heard Abby scream and then saw Lizzie wearing a rubber hood on her head. The story said that Lizzie "must have been standing over the mutilated remains of her mother at the very time that her father was about to enter the house."[90]

Edward McHenry claimed to have heard much of what he told Trickey while lying under Lizzie's bed in her cell. Of course the detective had made it all up, and people soon called the *Globe* to dispute what McHenry claimed they had said. Within a day of publishing the story, the *Globe* realized it had been duped. On October 11 it issued an apology to its readers and to Lizzie. Saying it had been misled, it regretted adding "to the terrible burden of Miss Borden" and "for any injustice the publication of Monday inflicted upon her."[91]

The *New York Times* published most of the apology and noted that most people thought this incident weakened the state's case against Lizzie. For one thing, hiring an outside detective seemed to suggest that Fall River police did not have faith in their own detective work. The *Globe* story said as much. For another, the men who would form the grand jury would have certainly read about the false story against Lizzie. The article, the *Times* wrote, was leading to changing feelings about Lizzie's guilt, with more people now supporting her.

THE GRAND JURY DECIDES

ON NOVEMBER 15, the grand jury met for the first time. Breaking with usual arrangements for a grand jury, Hosea Knowlton invited Andrew Jennings to present witnesses who could speak in Lizzie's defense. Jennings declined. Edwin Porter, among others, thought that Knowlton's gesture showed how fair he was trying to be in the case, even as Lizzie's defenders attacked him and the police for supposedly trying to convict an innocent woman. So for one week the twenty-one jurors heard the state present its evidence against Lizzie. They didn't have to all reach the same decision, as in a court trial. If eleven jurors thought Lizzie should face trial, she would.

The grand jury testimony ended on November 21, with the jurors not reaching a decision. In the days that followed, the case against Lizzie took an unexpected turn. Her friend Alice Russell had testified at the grand jury proceedings, as she had at the inquest and the preliminary hearing. But after she testified in November, something began to eat at her. She had sworn to tell "the whole truth," but she had never publicly told anyone about an incident that happened in the Borden home on August 7. A lawyer she talked to after her grand jury appearance told her she should go back and tell all she knew.

Russell had stayed with Lizzie and Emma at the house since the day of the murders. On the morning of the seventh, Alice entered the kitchen to see the two sisters discussing a dress that Lizzie held. She told Emma she was going to burn it because it had paint on it. Lizzie then began to tear up the dress and put the pieces into the stove. (Bridget Sullivan later told reporters that the Borden family often got rid of old or unwanted clothes by burning them.)

Russell told her story to the grand jury on the morning of December 1. There's no way to know if what she said swayed the jury, but that afternoon it reached a decision. The state had presented enough evidence to convince twenty of the twenty-one jurors that Lizzie should go on trial for murder. And Lizzie and Alice Russell were no longer friends.

9

THE ROAD TO THE SUPERIOR COURT

The grand jurors spent about six hours reaching a decision. On December 2 they announced that Lizzie was being charged with three crimes: the murder of Andrew, the murder of Abby, and the murder of the pair. The verdict, Edwin Porter wrote, saddened the "thousands of people who maintained all along that the Fall River police, the Medical Examiner, the Judge of the District Court and the District Attorney had labored in vain" to charge Lizzie with the murders.[92]

Lizzie would go on trial in superior court in New Bedford, Massachusetts, sometime in 1893, though the state did not set a date, and would not for six months. Various theories arose as to why Hosea Knowlton and Attorney General Albert Pillsbury refused Andrew Jennings's repeated calls for them to set a date. Perhaps the state officials thought that Lizzie would mentally crack while in jail. She might confess to the crimes, or suffer some kind of breakdown that would make a trial unnecessary. Or perhaps neither Knowlton nor Pillsbury was eager to try the case, given Lizzie's growing support around the country. Pillsbury would have normally prosecuted such an important case, but he declined because of illness. That meant Knowlton would continue to try to prove Lizzie's guilt.

In the first days after the indictment was announced, the newspapers reported some of what jurors thought about the case. One supposedly said, "They'll hang her, sure."[93] Another told the *Boston Globe* that the government's witnesses "were reluctant, and acted as if they wanted to believe Lizzie Borden innocent."[94] Meanwhile, Emma Borden was so shocked and disappointed by her sister's indictment that she stayed in bed for several days.

And Lizzie, the *Fall River News* claimed, "though trying to bear up under the awful charges that confront her, is also much distressed."[95]

◆

WAITING FOR HER DAY IN COURT

KNOWING SHE WOULD go on trial but not when, Lizzie spent the Christmas and New Year's holidays in jail. From her cell, she heard the jingling of bells on the sleighs that raced over the winter snow. In mid-January she wrote another letter to her good friend Annie Lindsey. She had meant to write sooner, Lizzie said, "but my head troubles me so much I write very little." She wrote that maybe soon the officials would have to take her to the local insane asylum, as she tried to deal with being in jail and what was still to come. She went on, "I cannot for the life of me see how you and the rest of my friends can be so full of hope over the case. To me, I see nothing but the densest shadows."[96]

While Lizzie struggled with this bout of sadness, her defense team was hard at work. Andrew Jennings and Melvin Adams now had a third, and respected, lawyer to help them in court: George Robinson. Along with his legal career, Robinson was also a politician. He had served in Congress and had been governor of Massachusetts from 1884 to 1886. Before his election as governor, one Massachusetts paper praised him as the best of the state's congressmen and predicted he would be one of the state's best governors ever. At the time, Massachusetts governors served for only one year, so the state's voters liked him enough to elect him three years in a row.

By April, Knowlton knew he would be prosecuting the Borden case. Writing to Attorney General Pillsbury, he seemed unsure that he could convince a jury that Lizzie was guilty, though perhaps he could get a hung jury, meaning the jurors would split in their opinions over her guilt. That would end the trial, though the state could then try Lizzie again. In his own mind, though, Knowlton believed Lizzie had murdered her father and stepmother. Although Pillsbury would not take part in the case, Knowlton would be assisted by William Moody, who served as the district attorney for a county outside Boston. Moody, though, had little experience prosecuting criminal cases and had never taken part in a murder trial. His role in the Borden case won Moody his first national attention. He went on to become secretary of the navy under President Theodore Roosevelt and was named a US Supreme Court justice in 1906.

As Knowlton prepared for his case, he received letters from people as far away as Colorado with their views on what had happened. The letters had started arriving soon after the inquest. One man wanted to clear Lizzie's name and confessed to the murders. But the unnamed writer said, "No power Will Ever hang me for the Deed for I Shall Blow My Brains out." A judge from South Carolina wrote that he could cite "a long list of cases . . . where children have slain their parents."[97] Another wrote that in a vision, he or she saw bloody clothing hidden under a floorboard at 92 Second Street.

Around the same time that Knowlton expressed doubts about convicting Lizzie, the state finally set the date for her trial to begin: June 5. Before that, on May 8, Lizzie went to the New Bedford courthouse to be arraigned for her alleged crimes. She traveled there with Sheriff and Mrs. Wright. In the court, a paper reported, she showed "the same nerve and firmness that she exhibited . . . since the day of the murder."[98] The arraignment took only ten minutes. To each of the three charges of murder, Lizzie said, "I am not guilty."[99] She then returned to her Taunton cell.

Within a few days after the arraignment, Lizzie developed a fever and an infection in her lungs. The doctor who took care of patients at the jail had her moved to the Wrights' home so she could recover. During this time, Lizzie wrote again to Annie Lindsey. Her spirits were once again low. She wrote, "I see no ray of light amid the gloom. . . . My friend—do not make any plans for me at Christmas. I do not expect to be free—and if I am, I could not join in any merry making. I don't know that I ever could again, certainly not at present. You know my life can never be the same again if I ever come home." Lizzie apologized for the dark feelings she shared, "but my heart is heavy and the burden laid upon me seems greater than I can bear."[100]

THE REAL KILLER?

To supporters of Lizzie Borden, another ax murder that took place in Fall River offered some hope for her defense. On

May 30, 1893, Stephen Manchester returned from his rounds of delivering milk from the family farm to find his daughter Bertha lying in a pool of blood. Someone had taken an ax to her head, leaving the top of her skull crushed to a pulp. As fear once again gripped Fall River, some people wondered if Bertha's killer could have been the same person who murdered Andrew and Abby Borden.

This slaughter, however, was different from the Borden killings in several ways. For one, the murderer left the apparent murder weapon at the scene of the crime. For another, the murderer had stolen several items from Bertha. The Fall River police began questioning several men who had worked on the Manchester farm and learned that one of them had left the farm on bad terms with his boss. He became their prime suspect. Jose Correa deMello was a recent immigrant from the Azores. Apparently deMello was only planning to rob Bertha Manchester but killed her when she resisted him. DeMello was convicted and served twenty years in prison. Andrew Jennings, as the news of the murder first spread, asked reporters, "Well, are they going to claim that Lizzie Borden did this too?"[101] Jennings was making a biting joke, since he and everyone else knew Lizzie was in jail when Bertha was hacked more than twenty times. But deMello had his own alibi that proved he could not have killed Andrew and Abby—he had come to the United States after their murder.

THE TRIAL BEGINS

ON JUNE 3, Lizzie and Sheriff Wright took a carriage from the Bristol County Jail to the Taunton train station. To try to avoid drawing attention to them, Wright wore street clothes, not his uniform. Once on the train, the pair sat at the rear of their car, again hoping to avoid being seen. Lizzie read a magazine as the train chugged toward New Bedford.

Despite the attempt at staying out of the public eye, some newspaper reporters waited at the jail when Lizzie and Wright's carriage arrived there. The New Bedford jail keeper quickly opened the gate to the jail to let the carriage through and then just as quickly bolted it shut. Lizzie's new home for the length of the trial was called a hospital cell. It was about twice as big as the other cells in the jail. Once again, Lizzie was getting special treatment that other prisoners could not expect.

On the morning of June 5, just before eleven a.m., Lizzie arrived at the courthouse with Sheriff Wright by her side. The day was scorching hot, but Lizzie was dressed all in black, including her cotton gloves. A crowd of people, mostly women and young girls, stood outside. A reporter from the *Boston Globe* described how Lizzie looked. He said that the illustrations of her in the newspapers "have done her no justice at all. Some have made her out a hard and hideous fright, and others have flattered her. She is, in truth, a very plain-looking old maid." The reporter compared her to a schoolteacher, looking "plain" and "practical."[102]

Indicted on three counts of murder, Lizzie first faced trial on the count of murdering both Andrew and Abby. On this opening day of the trial, the public was not allowed inside, but reporters were. Lizzie saw some familiar faces as she entered the room.

They included her lawyers and District Attorney Knowlton, along with the two ministers from Fall River who had supported her from the beginning. As she came in, the *New York Times* reported, Lizzie's face flushed. The pink color, "those who have watched her have learned to know denotes excitement."[103] She then smiled as she greeted Jennings and Adams.

In charge of the trial were three judges, also called justices. The chief justice was Albert Mason. On either side of him sat Caleb Blodgett and Justin Dewey. The youngest of the three, Dewey, had a tie to defense attorney George Robinson. Dewey owed his job to Robinson, who had named the justice to the court during his term as governor.

The first day was devoted to selecting a panel of twelve jurors to decide Lizzie's guilt or innocence. Chief Justice Mason questioned the 145 potential jurors, trying to weed out anyone who had already formed a strong opinion on whether or not Lizzie was a murderer. Jurors would also be excused if they said they didn't support the death penalty, and some of the men interviewed held that position. Joe Howard, a well-known New York reporter covering the trial, said the potential jurors were "crowded, hot, uncomfortable and impatient to be about their work."[104] Each team of lawyers could also challenge the selection of a juror, up to twenty-two each, without giving a reason. If they wanted to challenge more, they had to present their reasons why to the court. The prosecution used just over half of these twenty-two challenges, while Jennings used all of his. Each time he suggested a challenge, Lizzie confirmed it.

Finally, as the hot day dragged on, the justices had found twelve men for the jury. None came from Fall River, though they lived in nearby towns in Bristol County. Half were farmers. Most were Protestants. The youngest juror, John Finn, was also the only one of Irish descent. The jurors, Joseph Conforti asserted in *Lizzie Borden on Trial*, were "men of steady habits and steady employment . . . and who surely held traditional views of Victorian womanhood."[105] Before the day ended, Chief Justice Mason informed the twelve jurors that they would be isolated from friends and family through the course of the trial. The jurors then went off for half an hour and chose Charles I. Richards as their foreman.

The next day William Moody would present the state's opening statements, and then the jury would head to Fall River to inspect the crime scene. But before that trip took place, Lizzie showed one of her first public reactions to what was going on around her.

10

LIZZIE ON TRIAL

On the second day of the trial, dozens of spectators were allowed in the courtroom. Most were men, but some women attended too. Lizzie sat in the middle of the room; her position let half the crowd see her face, while the rest only saw her back. The court clerk read the charges against her and informed the jury that Lizzie had pleaded not guilty to all three counts of murder. Then William Moody approached the jurors and summarized the state's case against the accused.

The reporters covering the trial disagreed on how Moody appeared and spoke as he made the prosecution's opening statements. The *New York Times* commented on his "earnest and impressive air." The *Boston Globe* said the attorney "seemed very much constrained and ill at ease."[106] But several reporters agreed that Moody talked in a conversational tone as he described the Borden family, their house, and the cold relationship that had developed between Abby and Lizzie. He also described the events of August 4, 1892. Moody spoke for ninety minutes or more, with Lizzie staring intently at him most of the time.

June 6 was another hot day, and Lizzie held a fan as she sat in the stuffy courtroom. At times she waved it, trying to create a small cooling breeze. Other times, she put the folded fan into her mouth. And when Moody displayed the hatchet head broken off at the handle that the police had found, Lizzie opened the fan and covered her face with it.

As he finished, Moody reminded the jurors that they had to be guided only by the law and evidence presented in court. He asked them "to keep your minds in the same open attitude which you have maintained today" till the end of the trial. And if the evidence convinced them that Lizzie was guilty of murder, "we ask you in your verdict to declare her guilty."[107]

When Moody finished, Lizzie seemed to some observers to have fallen asleep. In reality she had fainted, though the onlookers could only guess why. Was it from the heat? Or was it from the mental strain of hearing Moody discuss the murders? Joe Howard reported that Lizzie caught a glimpse of her dead parents' skulls, which were part of the prosecution's evidence. Whatever had caused it, Lizzie's fainting spell filled the headlines of the articles describing the day's events. In the court, someone brought over smelling salts, a chemical mixture containing a form of ammonia. They were used to revive someone who had been knocked out or fainted, and they seemed to work on Lizzie. She was soon up and drinking some water.

The trial went on, and Moody called his first witness, an engineer who described the layout of the Borden house. Then, after a lunch break, the jurors went to see the house for themselves. Lizzie was given the option of going with them, but she declined. Back at her cell, she seemed completely recovered from her faint. She talked with the jailer about books. The jailer, the *Boston Globe* reported, had come to see Lizzie as a "sensible woman . . . calm yet of good spirits."[108]

A VERDICT FROM BEYOND?

One unsigned letter Hosea Knowlton received during the case against Lizzie came from someone who claimed to have used a Ouija board to get information about the murders. The board was first sold in 1891, and early ads called it "the wonderful talking board."[109] Like today's board, the original one had the letters of the alphabet and numbers on it, though it was made out of wood and not cardboard. During the latter part of the nineteenth century, some Americans believed in spiritualism, the idea that the spirits of dead people could contact the living. The makers of the Ouija board tapped into that belief, suggesting that players received answers to their questions from unseen spirits. The letter that Knowlton received said that the Ouija board asserted Lizzie had killed her parents. But when asked if she would be convicted, the board said "never."[110] The board also said Lizzie committed the murders wearing only pants and a hat! Some people had suggested, usually jokingly, that Lizzie committed the murders naked so she would not have to worry about getting blood on her clothes.

THE FIRST WITNESSES

HOSEA KNOWLTON AND William Moody called several witnesses on June 7, most notably Bridget Sullivan. Since the inquest hearing the previous August, she had lived and worked in New Bedford. She knew that some people in Fall River had suspected her of playing a role in the murders, but the police had never found any evidence against her. Lizzie's defense of Bridget may have helped end some of the suspicion against the maid, but not all.

For Bridget, many of the questions she faced were the same ones she had answered the day of the killings and during the previous legal proceedings. At the trial, she recounted her activities the morning of the murders from when she woke up at six fifteen until the discovery of the two bodies. Moody asked if she had seen anyone enter the house as she did her chores that morning. Other than Mr. Borden, when he returned from his errands, she had not. Moody then asked about a dress Lizzie owned. The prosecution believed that the one Lizzie had turned over to the police as evidence was not the same one she wore the morning of August 4, 1892. Bridget knew the dress that Moody mentioned, but she couldn't remember if Lizzie wore it or any other particular dress that morning.

That answer seemed to undercut the prosecution's argument that Lizzie had turned in a different dress, since they couldn't get this witness to confirm what she wore. Bridget's testimony again seemed to weaken the prosecution's case when she answered questions from defense lawyer George Robinson. He asked her, "You never saw any conflict in the family?" She replied, "No, sir."[111] That answer seemingly called into question the state's assertion of conflict between Abby and Lizzie. Yet Bridget did confirm that Emma and Lizzie didn't always eat with their father and mother.

The next day Bridget made another brief appearance, as the

defense wanted to clear up something that she had said at the inquest. Then, she had claimed that she saw Lizzie crying just minutes after finding her father's body. Now Bridget swore that she'd never seen Lizzie cry.

On June 8 Adelaide Churchill followed Bridget to the stand. Moody had better luck questioning her about the dress Lizzie wore the morning of the murders. She insisted that the dress Lizzie gave police and that Moody showed her in court was not the one Lizzie had on. She recalled Lizzie wearing a dress with some light blue in it. Yet under questioning by Robinson, the witness could not precisely describe what she thought Lizzie had worn.

The biggest buzz of the next day came when Alice Russell took the stand. People knew that Lizzie's old friend had finally come forward with testimony that suggested Lizzie tried to destroy evidence. Russell started off by recounting Lizzie's visit to her house on the third, when Lizzie expressed her fears about someone trying to harm the family. Then she moved on to what she saw when she came to the house after the murder and during the time she stayed with Lizzie and Emma. Russell described seeing Lizzie burning a dress. She left the kitchen and then returned to see Lizzie taking another piece of the dress out of a kitchen cabinet and preparing to burn it, too.

No police were in the house at the time, but they were outside guarding it. Russell said that she told Lizzie, "I wouldn't let anyone see me do that, Lizzie." After the incident, Russell talked to Orrington Hanscom. He worked for a private detective agency. Emma and Lizzie had hired him to investigate the case. Hanscom asked Russell if all the dresses that had been in the house the day of the murder were still there. Russell lied and said yes. The next day she told Lizzie that the worst thing she could have done was burn the dress and that she had been questioned about Lizzie's dresses. Lizzie replied, "Oh, what made you let me do it?"[112]

Under further questioning, Russell said she didn't know what dress Lizzie was wearing the morning of the fourth. But the dress she saw Lizzie burn matched the description of the dress Adelaide Churchill said she saw Lizzie wear that morning. Lizzie had told Emma she was burning the dress because it had paint on it. The prosecution was suggesting that Lizzie burned it because the stain was blood and she was trying to get rid of the evidence.

As Russell spoke, Lizzie showed little emotion or interest in what she said. Later, when Assistant Marshal John Fleet testified, she remained seemingly uninterested, but the clanging together of the axes and hatchets the police had found made her jump. Fleet spent most of his time describing the police's searches of the Borden home on the fourth and the sixth. Under questioning from Robinson, he admitted that he did not see a dress with either paint or blood on it. On the whole, he said, the search of Lizzie's room was not as thorough as it should have been. With this and other questioning, Robinson was trying to show that the police had not done their job properly. And if that were the case, how could they be so sure that Lizzie had committed the murders?

Fleet returned to testify the next day, and Robinson continued to hammer away at the police search of the Borden home. When Robinson asked if the police had thoroughly checked two trunks in Lizzie's room, Fleet said they had not. Robinson then turned to the broken hatchet found in the basement. Fleet said he had not taken out the handle. But Officer Michael Mullaly later testified that Fleet had taken the handle out of the box it lay in and then put it back in. Fleet was called back to the stand and insisted he had not taken out the piece of the handle and put it back. Other officers backed Fleet's account, but the incident, the *New York Times* reported, elated the defense, and other papers played up how the officers contradicted one another. Joe Howard, who didn't show much kindness toward the Fall River police, wrote that all the officers were certain of everything they saw and heard at the Borden home. "There hasn't been an officer on the stand who has not been absolutely confident, nor has there been one who has not been flatly contradicted by one of his associates."[113]

POINTS SCORED BY BOTH SIDES

HIGHLIGHTING CONTRADICTIONS BY the police helped the defense weaken the state's case. But it won its first major victory on June 12. That day the judges accepted the defense's arguments not to let the state introduce Lizzie's inquest testimony. The issue revolved around whether Lizzie was under arrest when she testified. The state argued that she was a suspect at the time, but not under arrest. She had spoken voluntarily at the inquest, and Andrew Jennings had told her she did not have to testify. The judges decided that even though Lizzie had not been arrested for the murders, she was "practically in custody."[114] The judges ruled that meant her statements at the time were not voluntary—she felt compelled to give them, and so they could not be entered into the trial. This decision meant that the jurors would never hear Lizzie's own contradictions about what she had done on the morning of August 4. Sitting in court and hearing this news, Lizzie began to cry. At least one onlooker assumed they were tears of relief.

But as the day went on, Lizzie was clearly distressed by some of the testimony she heard. Dr. Dolan gave details about the condition of Abby and Andrew's bodies when he arrived at the crime scene. He described the wounds they'd received from the weapon that killed them and his cutting off the heads to preserve them as evidence. The testimony upset Lizzie, and for a time that day and the next, she left the courtroom. She stayed in a room nearby, so she could still hear the testimony but did not have to see any gruesome evidence.

Another medical witness showed that the hatchet head without a handle fit several of the wounds in Andrew's skull. Could that hatchet have been the murder weapon? Knowlton asked. This witness and a doctor who followed him to the stand said yes. The experts also said that the deadly hatchet blows could have been made by a woman.

As the trial went on, the reporters covering it continued to note Lizzie's condition each day, along with what she wore. On Monday, June 12, Joe Howard reported, "her color was bad, her manner listless."[115] Several newspapers noted that she had spent time over the weekend reading a book by Charles Dickens. She had no visitors in her cell, except for her legal team, but she did receive letters from friends. Her appetite, it was reported, was good. In the courtroom, she sometimes greeted the friends who came out to support her. Annie Lindsey was there a few times, and she held her old friend's hand as the testimony went on.

On June 13 the state's medical experts continued their testimony. The tiny blood spot found on Lizzie's clothing, Joe Howard reported, was labeled natural. The experts said that except for that spot and the blood on the carpets, none of the suspicious spots examined were blood. Melvin Adams of the defense got Dr. David Cheever to admit that normally slicing a body's arteries would lead to a lot of blood splattering the attacker. But Knowlton drew out from the doctor that someone could wear something over their clothing to keep it from getting covered in blood.

The prosecution called its last witnesses on June 14. They included Hannah Reagan, the matron at the Fall River police station. Under oath, she repeated what she said she had heard almost a year before, when Emma came to visit Lizzie. The jurors heard that Lizzie said to her sister, "Emma, you have given me away, haven't you?" and Emma denied it.[116] Then the prosecution called drugstore clerk Eli Bence to the stand to testify about seeing Lizzie in his store the day before the murders.

Bence, however, only got to say a few words before George Robinson stood up and asked the justices not to let the clerk testify. At this point, the jury and the witnesses left the courtroom so the two legal teams could argue about whether Bence should be allowed to testify. Moody cited earlier court decisions that he said showed that Bence should be allowed to speak. If Lizzie had tried to buy the prussic acid, it could show that she was already thinking about killing her parents. The prosecution also wanted to show that Lizzie's stated intent to buy it—to clean a sealskin cape—was not a generally accepted use of the acid. Robinson argued that trying to buy poison had nothing to do with eventually killing someone with an ax. The justices conferred for about an hour, then decided that Bence could perhaps testify. But he could do so only after experts testified about the uses of prussic acid. What they said would shape whether or not the justices thought the prussic acid was relevant to the case.

The prosecution called those experts the next day, but the defense objected to many of the answers. Chief Justice Mason often ruled in its favor, meaning the testimony was not allowed. After four witnesses appeared to speak about prussic acid, Mason ruled that Bence would not be allowed to testify after all. With that, the prosecution rested its case. Now it would be Lizzie's lawyers' turn to call witnesses. They would try to poke holes in the state's case and show it had not proven Lizzie guilty of killing Andrew and Abby.

11

THE VERDICT COMES DOWN

After the court ruled that Eli Bence could not testify, Chief Justice Mason ordered a short recess. Lizzie and several of her friends stood and chatted, sometimes laughing as they spoke. When the trial began again, Andrew Jennings began to present Lizzie's defense. He talked about his personal relationship with the Borden family and having known Lizzie for many years. He said that who killed the

Bordens was a mystery, but it wasn't up to the jurors to determine who did it. They simply had to decide if the state had proven that Lizzie did it. And Jennings was confident that the state had failed in its task.

He argued that Lizzie did not have a motive. Bridget Sullivan, who spent more time with the family than any other outsider, had said the Bordens got along. And while one witness testified that Lizzie complained about her stepmother, there was no evidence to show that she had bad relations with her father. Jennings said, "There was nothing whatever between this father and this daughter that should cause her to do such a wicked, wicked act as this." He said all the state presented was circumstantial evidence. But in this case, he said, "There is not a spot of blood, there is not a weapon that they have connected with her in any way, shape or fashion. . . . There is not, I say, a particle of direct testimony in the case connecting her with this crime."[117] The *Boston Herald* reported that "his belief in her innocence shone in his words like a loving light in a forest."[118] At times, Lizzie cried as Jennings made his remarks.

MYSTERIOUS PEOPLE AND SOUNDS

JENNINGS THEN BEGAN calling a number of witnesses who said they saw or heard strange things around the Borden house before the murders. Two neighbors said they heard a pounding noise coming from outside the house on the night of August 3. A resident on Third Street not far away saw a stranger sleeping on their steps that night. Several people, including Benjamin Handy, saw strangers at or near the Borden house on the morning of the fourth. Handy again recounted seeing the same unknown man by the house two times before ten thirty. Jennings had no proof that any of these strangers had played any role in the murders. But all he had to do was get the jury thinking that one of them, and not Lizzie, could have killed the Bordens.

Other witnesses testified about what they saw just before the murders or after they were discovered. An ice cream seller named Hyman Lubinsky had driven his carriage down Second Street just after eleven a.m. He had sold ice cream to the Bordens before and knew the house, though he didn't know Lizzie. Lubinsky said that he saw a woman in a dark dress go from the Bordens' barn and head for the house. That seemed to confirm Lizzie's explanation of being in the barn just before discovering her father's body. Charles Sawyer, the neighbor who stood guard at the Bordens' side door after the murders, was one of the first people on the scene on the fourth. He testified that he did not see any blood on Lizzie and that she was obviously distressed by the murders.

The defense also called two teenagers who said they had entered the Bordens' barn after the murders but before the police did. They claimed to have gone in to look for the murderer, though as Hosea Knowlton pointed out, the barn was latched from the outside. Someone hiding in the barn could not have locked themselves in like that. Their presence in the barn, though, suggested that the police had failed to do their job. The boys or someone else could have accidentally tampered with evidence there.

The day ended, Joe Howard reported, with the defense team feeling good about their chances to free Lizzie. Howard seemed to share their belief in successfully defending her. He wrote, "There is no reasonable expectancy of any verdict save one of 'not guilty.'"[119]

The next day, June 16, Lizzie sat with her lawyers. She had not slept well the night before, but she seemed to be in good spirits. The courtroom was once again packed, as it had been throughout the trial. Jennings began the day by calling several witnesses who contradicted the testimony of Hannah Reagan, the matron at the Fall River police station. These witnesses included journalists who had questioned Reagan after she claimed she had heard Emma and Lizzie arguing over what Emma told Jennings. They said that Reagan denied hearing the supposed quarrel or telling a reporter she had.

Of all the witnesses who refuted Reagan's testimony, the one most people in the court were eager to hear was Emma Borden. Along with denying the matron's claim of Lizzie arguing with her, Emma also said that she had encouraged her sister to burn the dress, because it was "very dirty, very much soiled and badly faded."[120]

When Knowlton questioned Emma, he pointed out inconsistencies between what she had said at the inquest and what she was now telling the jury. She had previously said that relations between the sisters and their stepmother were not cordial after the incident with the house on Fourth Street. But in court she said Abby and Lizzie had been on good terms for the last three years. Emma also told the prosecutor that Lizzie and Alice Russell were not close friends. Yet minutes after Lizzie knew her father was dead, she sent for Alice, and she stayed in the Borden house for four days. Recalling the dress-burning incident, Emma seemed to have some trouble remembering who said what when. She also described how Alice said she had lied to Orrington Hanscom when he asked her about the dresses in the house. Alice had said all of them were still there, when she knew Lizzie had burned one. Emma claimed that she and Lizzie told Alice to tell Hanscom she had lied—a detail that had never emerged in Alice's version of the story.

The defense rested its case that afternoon. Lizzie did not appear on the stand. Her lawyers said that "there is nothing new which would be brought out by her testimony" and she was "already worn and unfit to stand the severe strain to which her presence on the stand would subject her to."[121] Jennings and his team also did not want to give the state the chance to bring up Lizzie's inquest testimony. The defense had long claimed that

that testimony was clouded by the painkillers Lizzie had gotten from Dr. Bowen after the murders. But as Knowlton had brought out earlier, no one had actually seen Lizzie take the drugs.

ROBINSON'S LAST WORDS

SINCE IT WAS Friday, Lizzie would have two days back in her cell to think about what would happen next. Various reporters covering the trial believed what Andrew Jennings had said when he opened his defense: lacking direct evidence against Lizzie, the state had not proven its case. As the *New York Times* pointed out, two decisions by the justices had weakened Hosea Knowlton's efforts. The first was denying the introduction of Lizzie's inquest testimony. The second was refusing to let Eli Bence testify. Still, overall the *Times* thought that the prosecution did not have enough solid evidence, and the identity of the murderer, the paper guessed, would remain a "baffling mystery."[122]

On Monday, June 19, the courtroom was once again packed as Lizzie took her seat. Near her sat Emma and their uncle John

Morse. George Robinson spoke first, taking about four hours to argue for Lizzie's innocence. He started by admitting that the murder of Andrew and Abby Borden was "one of the most dastardly and diabolical of crimes that was ever committed in Massachusetts." Robinson argued that only someone "whose heart is blackened with depravity . . . a maniac or fiend we say" could have murdered the Bordens.[123]

He then reminded the jurors that they held Lizzie's life in their hands. If they convicted her, she could face the death penalty. He often referred to her as "Miss Lizzie" or "the girl," trying to create an image of someone who by nature was young and innocent—and not a calculating murderer.

As he spoke, Robinson stressed details that the police could not agree on, and the discredited tale of Hannah Reagan. The lawyer said that the Fall River police felt a pressure to arrest someone and turned to Lizzie because of the weak circumstantial evidence they had gathered. Police, Robinson said, are not perfect, and they make mistakes. By suspecting Lizzie over anyone else, he suggested, the Fall River force had made a huge one. And he asked the jurors how they would feel if a man, even a police officer, went into their daughters' rooms and began questioning them, as Assistant Marshal Fleet had done with Lizzie. Robinson was playing to the Victorian ideas about the proper relations between men and women and was suggesting Fleet had violated them.

Robinson then offered his own theory on what might have happened on the morning of August 4. Some unknown person entered the Borden house, looking to kill Andrew. He found Abby instead and murdered her, then waited for Andrew to return home to kill him. But as Robinson told the jurors, the defense did not have to provide any evidence to support this idea. It was just one possible explanation for what happened.

Robinson also talked about Lizzie's good character, her religious faith, and her desire to help others. He pointed out that when Mayor Coughlin first said she was a suspect, Lizzie was ready to go then or anytime for questioning. "Gentlemen," Robinson said, "murderers do not talk that way." He then asked the jurors what they had seen in Lizzie as they watched her every day in court. "Have you seen anything that shows the lack of human feeling and womanly bearing?" Robinson reminded the jurors one last time about the great responsibility they held.

To find Lizzie guilty, each of them had to be sure beyond a reasonable doubt that she had murdered Andrew and Abby. If they convicted her without the state having proven Lizzie's guilt, then the jurors would be committing "so deplorable an evil that the tongue can never speak its wickedness."[124]

Throughout Robinson's long speech, Lizzie watched him carefully, following every word. The only time she cried, Joe Howard reported, was when her attorney mentioned the tiny gold ring Lizzie had given her father years before. He wore that ring the day he was murdered, and he was buried with it. Robinson wanted to show the close bond between the father and daughter, to suggest that Lizzie had no reason to kill this man she loved.

THE PROSECUTION ARGUES ITS CASE

HOSEA KNOWLTON BEGAN his final statement just after three p.m. He admitted the case was not an easy one for either side to argue in court. "It was an incredible crime," he said, and the woman accused of it was not the typical criminal. She was a lady, "the equal of your wife and mine . . . of whom such things had never been suspected or dreamed before."[125] But Knowlton had the duty to go over the facts he and William Moody had presented that convinced them Lizzie was guilty.

The district attorney reminded the jurors that literature and history had plenty of examples of women who committed terrible crimes. One such crime had happened in Massachusetts just a few years before, and Sarah Jane Robinson had been convicted of murdering several people. He noted that men of that era were raised to believe that women were pure, and prosecuting Lizzie had been "the saddest duty of my life."[126] The jurors, like Knowlton, had to put aside the fact that Lizzie was a woman. Unlike Robinson, Knowlton did not want the jurors to see Lizzie as some helpless girl. He made a point of referring to her as "this woman," "the defendant," or by her full name.

Knowlton argued that Abby Borden, not her father, was the real target of Lizzie's brutality. And he denied the defense's claim that a murderer could have entered and freely moved about the house, given how many doors the Bordens kept locked. As he talked about the evidence the state had presented, he at times referred to Lizzie as a murderer and liar. Joe Howard said that as Knowlton spoke, he walked back and forth, moving his hands as he made points, and turned his gaze from the jurors to the justices, then from Lizzie to the crowd eager to hear his every word.

The day ended with Knowlton still speaking, and he picked up his closing arguments the next day. He went on to explain why Lizzie might have murdered her father. After killing Abby, she knew he would suspect that she was the killer. "He knew [Lizzie] disliked her. He knew who could not tolerate her presence under the roof."[127] Knowlton stressed that Abby had no enemies in the world. Only her stepdaughter showed hatred for her.

As to the defense, Knowlton said they presented "nothing," just "some dust thrown in our faces" and "absurd and trifling stories" about strange men around the Borden home.[128] Knowlton believed that the facts the state had presented showed that Lizzie had a reason to kill Abby, and the opportunity to do so.

When Knowlton finished, the court recessed for lunch. The trial began again at one forty-five, and for the first and only time,

Lizzie spoke in the courtroom. Chief Justice Mason said she could say whatever she chose to the jury. Lizzie simply said, "I am innocent. I leave it to my counsel to speak for me."[129] Justice Dewey then delivered the charge—the instructions for the jury to follow as they considered whether or not Lizzie was guilty.

Even to someone who was not a lawyer, like reporter Joe Howard, the charge was "remarkable; it was a plea for the innocent."[130] Judges should not reveal any feelings about how they view the evidence presented in a case before them, but Dewey did. He asked the jurors if some young women didn't sometimes "use words which . . . would go far beyond their real meaning."[131] He said this while discussing testimony presented about Lizzie saying she disliked her stepmother. He then questioned the note Abby supposedly received to go visit a friend. The prosecution said Lizzie had made up that story, but Dewey suggested Lizzie didn't have a reason to lie. He seemed to put more weight on the defense's suggestion that the real murderer had taken the note from the Borden home. Dewey's charge, Howard wrote, caused "smiles of joy to play about the lips of Lizzie's friends."[132] Lizzie, though, showed no emotion.

THE VERDICT

AFTER DEWEY'S CHARGE, the jury left the courtroom to decide Lizzie's fate. Few spectators left, as they assumed the jury would not need much time to make a decision—and they were right. Just a little more than an hour later, the twelve men filed back into the courtroom. The clerk of the court told Lizzie to stand, and she did. The foreman then passed papers to the clerk with the jury's verdict. The clerk instructed the foreman to look at Lizzie and Lizzie to look at him while he delivered his verdict. Before the clerk could finish speaking, the foreman interrupted him: "Not guilty."[133]

The courtroom erupted in cheers as Lizzie fell back down into her chair and began to cry. Andrew Jennings looked close to tears too, and someone heard him turn to Melvin Adams and say, "Thank God."[134] Hosea Knowlton asked that the remaining two murder charges against Lizzie be dismissed, and the justices agreed. Lizzie's long legal battle was over.

Lizzie spent the next hour sitting in the justices' private

rooms so she could calm herself. Then she took a carriage to the New Bedford train station so she could make her way back to Fall River. She said, "I want to see the old place and settle down at once."[135] The old place, though, might not have been the most welcoming. Since August 4, 1892, the crime scene had been left just as it was that morning. Now Emma and Lizzie could finally clean up the bloody mess in the sitting room and upstairs guest room.

In Fall River, people had waited anxiously to learn the verdict. The *New York Times* reported that the verdict surprised some of Lizzie's supporters; many thought the trial would end with a hung jury. When the news of the verdict reached the city, "the greatest excitement prevailed" as everyone talked about it.[136] People began to fill the streets in front of the Borden home, waiting to see Lizzie return. Instead, around eight fifteen she arrived at the nearby home of Charles Holmes. He had been a longtime friend of Andrew Borden and was the uncle of Lizzie's childhood friend Lulie Stillwell. Holmes and his family had supported Lizzie publicly throughout the trial.

Lizzie, along with Emma, entered the house. A reporter was allowed inside, and Lizzie told him she was "the happiest woman in the world."[137] She refused to talk about the trial, and she said she would stay at the Holmeses' for the night, given the crowd outside 92 Second Street. By ten p.m., some two thousand people filled the street there.

The question now on everyone's mind was, what would Lizzie do next? A restful vacation seemed in order, and Lizzie did spend some time in Newport, Rhode Island. After she returned, the jurors presented her with a picture of them taken after the trial. She wrote a letter to each juror, and in one she said she was grateful to have a photo "of the honest men who gave me my liberty."[138]

People wrote to her in turn, expressing their good wishes. She turned down at least one offer to speak about the trial in public. She also had reporters watching her movements for a time, even reporting when she walked downtown to run an errand. Some of Lizzie's friends, and probably Lizzie herself, hoped she could return to a quiet life. Going through the trial and proving her innocence was meant to be one step in that process. As George Robinson said right after the trial, Lizzie had thought going to trial "was the best thing, for when once she had finished it she knew that no one could rightfully accuse her of the crime."[139]

Rightly or wrongly, plenty of people still remained convinced of Lizzie's guilt even after the jurors said she had not killed Andrew and Abby Borden.

FALSE REPORTS OF A CONFESSION

Soon after Lizzie Borden was cleared of murdering her parents, she, Emma, and their friend Mary Ella Brigham traveled to Taunton to visit Mary Jane Wright. She and her husband, Sheriff Andrew Wright, had treated Lizzie kindly when she was locked up in the county jail there. (Mr. Wright was also present in the courtroom through Lizzie's trial. He served as bailiff, which meant his job was to keep the crowd quiet in the court.) Somehow this social visit to Taunton led to a wild rumor in the newspapers. While Lizzie and the other two women were on the train, the Associated Press released a report saying Lizzie had confessed to the murders. The story said that she was on her way to Taunton to turn herself in. The story was not true, but it showed the willingness of some reporters to believe any rumors they heard about one of the most famous women in America.

—————————————————————————

12

LIZZIE IN HER HOMETOWN

After the trial, Lizzie's fame made her the focus of many news reports and the curiosity of Fall River residents. Even tourists came to the city, to gawk outside 92 Second Street. Local reporters wrote about her visit to Fall River stores, and on at least one of those trips, store clerks came out into the streets and people went to their windows to follow Lizzie's movements. Some reporters also commented on what she wore. In one story, she was criticized for not wearing black after the murders, to show she was mourning the loss of her parents. No one expected her to mourn for Abby, "but common courtesy would suggest it in memory of her father."[140]

One of the first things Lizzie and Emma did was buy a new house. They must have been eager to leave behind the awful memories tied to their old one. For Lizzie, buying a new home also meant finally moving to the Hill, the wealthiest neighborhood in Fall River. After looking at several places, the sisters bought the house at 7 French Street. Lizzie later named her new home Maplecroft. It was only four years old and had all the modern conveniences of the time, including complete indoor plumbing. The three-story house also had a spiral staircase, stained-glass windows, and fine oak doors and trim. It was not the grandest house on French Street, but it was certainly a step up from the one Lizzie and Emma had left behind. And the sisters could afford it. With their father's death, they inherited an estate worth around $350,000—a huge sum of money in 1893. Since Abby died before Andrew, her estate passed to him and then to the sisters. Lizzie and Emma gave Abby's small estate, about $4,000, to Abby's surviving family members.

With all that was on their minds in the weeks after the trial, Lizzie and Emma dealt with one last gruesome detail of the murders. The state still possessed Andrew's and Abby's skulls, the flesh removed almost a year before by Medical Examiner William Dolan. At some point, the sisters asked Andrew Jennings to contact Hosea Knowlton to see about getting the skulls back. On July 14 Knowlton wrote Dolan that Jennings "insisted" the skulls be returned to Lizzie and Emma. Since there was no other case that would require the skulls as evidence, Knowlton wrote, "I see no reason why they should not be returned." What happened next is not clear, but Michael Martins and Dennis A. Binette, in *Parallel Lives: A Social History of Lizzie A. Borden and Her Fall River*, suggested that Dolan returned the skulls and the sisters quietly had them placed in their parents' grave at Oak Grove Cemetery. The authors reasoned that it was not likely "that the women would have had the desire to retain the grisly relics for any other purpose."[141]

MORE REACTIONS TO THE VERDICT

AS LIZZIE AND Emma tried to return to a private life, people in Massachusetts and beyond continued to focus on the murders. Some of the people who had publicly defended her before voiced their approval of the verdict. These included Susan Fessenden of the Woman's Christian Temperance Union and suffragist Mary Livermore. Livermore sent Lizzie a telegram saying "everybody is rejoicing" with the news of her acquittal.[142] But both of those prominent supporters wondered if Lizzie would always face suspicion from some people who still believed she was guilty.

As before and during the trial, newspapers had strong and differing opinions about the verdict. The *New York Times* had generally suggested all along that Lizzie was innocent. After the trial, it called Lizzie "a most unfortunate and cruelly persecuted woman" and noted that "there was never any serious reason to suppose that she was guilty."[143] The paper blamed the police for suspecting Lizzie when then they had no strong evidence against her.

The *Fall River Daily Globe* had been against Lizzie almost from the start, and it found fault with the verdict. Starting that August 4, the paper began a tradition of marking the anniversary of Andrew and Abby Borden's murder. That first year, it said "the murderer is free to walk the street, or visit the scene of the carnage."[144] The paper probably meant Lizzie, or it could have meant that the Fall River police had not identified any other suspects. After Lizzie's trial, the police had closed the case, so none ever would be.

People also reached out to Lizzie directly. She received many letters from supporters, though also some from people who still believed she was a murderer. She was not the only one to receive mail. Hosea Knowlton won praise from some lawyers for his closing argument in the case. Other people, though, still upset that he'd tried Lizzie at all, threatened him with violence.

In Fall River some of the people who stood with Lizzie through the trial did not remain as friendly afterward. Some members of the Central Congregational Church and its Christian Endeavor Society kept their distance from Lizzie. So did members of the local Young Woman's Christian Temperance

Union, which Lizzie had been part of before the murders. She and the group had a disagreement over a room the YWCTU rented for its meetings in the A. J. Borden building. With their father's death, the Borden sisters now controlled the building. The dispute played out in the local press, with the anti-Lizzie *Fall River Daily Globe* accusing Lizzie of kicking the group out of the building because some of its members had turned against her. The *Fall River Daily Evening News*, which supported Lizzie, said the dispute was over who would pay for repairs to the meeting room. That paper said Lizzie had not asked the group to leave the building. But the *Evening News* also reported that Lizzie felt some of her former friends in the group had given her a "cold and cutting reception."[145]

At one point the *Evening News* asked its readers, "Isn't it about time for the public to leave Lizzie Borden alone, and allow her to continue, undisturbed, her necessarily blemished and saddened life?"[146] For some youth of Fall River, the answer was clearly no. Over the years Lizzie made reports to the police about children throwing small stones or eggs at her house, or calling her names when she went outside. In church, people refused to sit near her, and she stopped going to Central Church or any other in Fall River.

If Lizzie cut back on some public appearances in Fall River, she didn't become a prisoner in Maplecroft. In October 1893 she traveled with two friends to the World's Columbian Exposition in Chicago. The fair marked the four hundredth anniversary of Christopher Columbus's first voyage to the Americas in 1492, though the fair didn't officially open until 1893. At the fair, people saw the world's first Ferris wheel and got to sample Juicy Fruit chewing gum for the first time. Lizzie and her friends paid fifty cents to attend the fair, which featured exhibits from more than forty nations.

At times when she traveled, Lizzie used a fake name, but she still could not always escape the attention of reporters. A news report from 1895 said that she traveled through Pittsfield, in western Massachusetts, on her way to nearby Stockbridge. The next year, the *Fall River Daily Evening News* reported that she visited Niagara Falls with Emma and their former neighbor on Second Street, Phebe Bowen. Lizzie also took trips to Boston, New York, and Washington to go shopping and see plays.

DAILY LIFE AT MAPLECROFT

THE CONTINUING ATTENTION Lizzie received after the trial at times made her suspicious of strangers. Early in 1894 a man visited the house while Lizzie was there alone. She didn't answer the door, as George Robinson had told her that reporters might try to harass her. The man left a card saying he was a friend of Lizzie's good friend Annie Lindsey. Lizzie wrote Annie about the incident and said that three times in the recent past, people had said Mary Livermore had sent them, when in fact the suffragist had not sent anyone to Maplecroft. In the letter, Lizzie apologized if the man really was a friend of Annie's. "I am very, very sorry if he is your friend, and hope you will tell him *why* I did not come down. Your friends are welcome when I am sure and I dislike to be discourteous to any one." Lizzie said she would gladly welcome the man if he came again, if he were really Annie's friend. She then told Annie about another visitor she had received, Annie's sister Ella. The two women shared a good time, but Lizzie felt moved to write, "I have so few friends here in Fall River."[147]

Although Lizzie might have lost some old friends, she made new ones after moving to the Hill. One of the closest was Emma Lake, who lived across the street. She and her husband, Edward, believed Lizzie was innocent and did not let the past influence how they treated her. The two women visited each other's homes, and Lizzie began to give Emma gifts to show how much she appreciated their friendship.

Emma's son Russell, who was born in 1895, often went over with his mother to visit Lizzie. He recalled years later that "as a child and later as a young man, [Lizzie] was just as nice and kind an old lady as one could ask for." When he opened a stand to sell lemonade, Lizzie was his first customer, and before Russell went away to boarding school, Lizzie gave him fifty cents. While some neighborhood children remembered Lizzie shouting at them, "Get out of my yard!" Russell was one of the privileged kids who could cut through it when he needed to, to escape a bully chasing him. Other children, Russell said, took on the views of their parents. If the adults disliked Lizzie, then the children "treated Miss Borden and her house like she was a witch or some person to fear and the house was haunted or a place to keep away from."[148]

Not all the children on the Hill, however, had such fond memories of Lizzie. Victoria Lincoln was one of the children whose parents still believed Lizzie had killed Andrew and Abby. She said children her age were "supposed to shudder and giggle when Miss Borden's name was mentioned." Despite believing that Lizzie had killed her parents, Victoria remembered trying to talk to her neighbor when Lizzie was outside filling her bird feeders. Lizzie, though, Victoria wrote years later, "never quite seemed to see or hear me," which stopped them from having a conversation. Like Lizzie, Victoria was the daughter of a success-ful bank president. Unlike her, Victoria lived all her childhood on the Hill. When it came to Lizzie's guilt, most people in the neighborhood "had no doubt that she did it."[149]

When she wasn't traveling or visiting with friends, Lizzie managed the people who helped take care of Maplecroft. She had a maid, a cook, and a coachman, who drove the carriage that took her and Emma around town. He also helped take care of the yard. Later the sisters hired a second maid. The two also met at times with Charles Cook, who handled their business affairs. That included helping them run the buildings they now owned and buying Maplecroft. Cook had helped Andrew Borden run his properties as well. In later years, he would arrange for Lizzie to buy more property on French Street next to Maplecroft.

While in the weeks after her acquittal Lizzie was often seen around Fall River, sometimes driving her own carriage, she made fewer trips as the years passed. But she could not end rumors or the public's interest in her life. In December 1896 many people in Fall River and across the country were surprised to read that Lizzie was about to get married. At thirty-six, Lizzie had never shown much interest in men and her status as a spinster seemed set for life. But the *Fall River Daily Globe* reported a rumor that Lizzie was preparing to marry "a Mr. Gardner of Swansea" and that a dressmaker was making fancy clothes for Lizzie for a planned European trip.[150] The Mr. Gardner referred to was apparently Orrin Gardner, a distant cousin of the Borden sisters. The rumor, though, proved to be just that. The *Fall River Daily Evening News* reported the next day that it had been authorized to deny the story. It's likely that Lizzie or someone close to her told the newspaper to deny the rumor.

The incident, though, upset Lizzie. She wrote her dressmaker,

Emma Cummings, to assure her that she didn't think Cummings had started the rumor. Lizzie then added, "Of course I am feeling very badly about [the story] but I must just bear as I have in the past."[151] The next year would see Lizzie once again bearing public attention she would prefer not to receive.

13

DIFFICULT YEARS

When Lizzie Borden traveled out of town, she sometimes went on shopping trips. With her inheritance, she could afford to buy nice things for herself and her house. And when she traveled, she enjoyed staying in fine hotels. Given her wealth, it must have surprised some people in Fall River—but not all—when Lizzie was accused of shoplifting.

The alleged incident happened in Providence, where many

wealthy Fall River residents went for special shopping trips. Lizzie was a customer at Tilden, Thurber & Company, which sold jewelry and silver items, among other things. After one of her visits to the store, two small paintings were discovered to be missing. In one version of the story, a woman who was friendly with the Borden sisters came into the store to have a small painting on porcelain repaired. The clerk realized that the painting was one the store carried in its stock, though the woman hadn't bought it there. The clerk then discovered that another painting like it was also gone. The customer said the painting needing repair had been a gift from Lizzie.

That led Tilden, Thurber to call in the police. A Providence detective went to Fall River to question Lizzie. The second missing painting was at Maplecroft. Lizzie claimed to have bought both paintings, though she said she paid much less than what the store said they were worth. The Providence police sought a warrant for Lizzie's arrest for stealing the two paintings, though it was never served. Apparently she made an arrangement with the store to cover the true cost of the paintings.

While this story didn't make headlines across the country, it was front-page news in the *Fall River Daily Globe*. And it helped fuel the rumors that Lizzie was a kleptomaniac. People said that when Andrew Borden was alive, local shopkeepers sent him bills after Lizzie left their stores without paying for items. Similar tales spread about stores sending bills to Lizzie's home in the years after she moved to Maplecroft. Mary Gifford, the wife of one Fall River store owner, said her husband and his staff always watched Lizzie closely when she came into his jewelry store. There is no evidence that Lizzie did shoplift from local stores, just these rumors. But the stories show that some residents were ready to believe the worst about Lizzie.

The rumors continued, even as she tried to avoid attention and quietly live her life. She bought more property on French Street. Her lifetime membership in a local animal protection league showed her interest in animals (though she sometimes complained to neighbors about their pets bothering her). She visited with her few close friends and their children. She made her frequent trips out of town. But the rumors kept coming, as some newspapers remained fascinated with Lizzie, probably thinking her name would help sell more copies.

During her time at Maplecroft, Lizzie often fed birds and she owned several dogs, and close friends often commented on her love of animals. But during her 1893 trial, at least two people wrote to Hosea Knowlton describing her violent treatment of cats. In one, the letter writer said she had heard stories in Boston of someone visiting the Bordens and being bothered by the family cat. Lizzie took the cat out of the room and later told the guest that the cat would never bother her again. When asked why, Lizzie supposedly said, "I've chopped its head off."[152] Variations of this story appeared over the years. In each case, the teller said that Lizzie chopped off the head of a cat or kitten. And in each case, the cat killings allegedly took place before the Borden murders, but they were not revealed until after Lizzie was arrested. Once again, Lizzie seemed to be the victim of anger or fear generated by the killings.

In 1899 the *Fall River Daily Evening News* reported on rumors that the state might put Lizzie on trial again. She could not be retried on the count of killing both Abby and Andrew, as the law does not allow someone to be tried for the same crime twice. But the state had not tried Lizzie on the separate count of killing Abby. The newspaper said that Lizzie could face trial for that, though Hosea Knowlton quickly dismissed the suggestion. Another rumor came out that private detectives had been following Lizzie after she was suspected of shoplifting in Boston. Lizzie probably never knew when her name would appear in the paper, tied to some rumor that was not true.

ONE RELATIONSHIP BEGINS, ANOTHER ENDS

GOING INTO THE twentieth century, one of Lizzie's favorite pastimes was going to the theater. Fall River had its own small theater, but Lizzie often traveled to Boston to see shows. Early in 1904 she saw a performance featuring Nance O'Neil, who was a well-known actress. After the show, Lizzie sent O'Neil flowers and a note, asking to meet her. O'Neil agreed, though she later claimed that at that time she did not know who Lizzie was. The two women soon became close friends. Their relationship also created more turmoil in Lizzie's life.

Later that year O'Neil performed at Fall River's Academy of Music. The show was so popular that the she returned a few weeks later, winning glowing reviews from the local papers. She and her acting troupe came back to the Spindle City several times in 1905. The two women deepened their friendship during O'Neil's stays in Fall River. O'Neil described Lizzie as someone who read a lot and showed great kindness, especially to animals. She was also, O'Neil said, someone who "seemed utterly lonely. . . . She was always so alone."[153]

With O'Neil, though, Lizzie found an eager friend, and she opened up her home at least once for a party for O'Neil and the other actors. Lizzie hired caterers to prepare food, and an orchestra provided entertainment. Victoria Lincoln was just a child at the time, but she heard that "the house blazed with lights from top to bottom and blared with music."[154]

Lizzie threw another party for O'Neil and her actor friends. O'Neil owned a home in the Massachusetts countryside near the New Hampshire border. Lizzie rented a house nearby and hosted a party that lasted a week. The fact that Lizzie paid for these parties and spent so much time with O'Neil fueled more rumors that have persisted to today: that the two women were lovers. Relations between people of the same sex were considered scandalous at the time, and not something most people talked about in public. Whatever relationship Lizzie and O'Neil had, it didn't seem to last much beyond 1906, when O'Neil ended her performances in New England.

By a few reports, some of Fall River's wealthy Yankee residents looked down on Lizzie's friendship with O'Neil and her fellow actors. One of them may have been her sister, Emma. In May 1905, Emma moved out of Maplecroft, and she and Lizzie were never close again. The *Boston Sunday Herald* reported that many people in Fall River blamed Lizzie's relationship with O'Neil for the split between the sisters. But disagreements between Lizzie and Emma, the paper said, were not new. They had earlier argued over Joseph Tetrault, who came to work for the sisters as a coachman in 1899. Once again, rumors, not hard facts, shape modern views of what happened while Tetrault was working for the Bordens. Some said that he and Lizzie had a sexual relationship. Whatever happened, Emma did not like Tetrault and wanted him fired. He did leave around 1903, though he came back shortly after that.

Emma's decision to leave the house and end her relationship with her sister didn't come after one explosive argument. It seems that she had been thinking about leaving for several years before finally doing it in 1905. Two years earlier she had discussed with Reverend Buck her concerns about staying with Lizzie. The minister, who had stood beside Lizzie during her trial, now told Emma she should leave Maplecroft.

In 1913 Emma talked about the split with Lizzie with the *Boston Sunday Post*. Exactly why she left, she said, "I must refuse to talk about. I did not go until conditions became absolutely unbearable." But even though she vowed not to return to Maplecroft as long as Lizzie lived there, Emma still felt she owed her sister something. She said she would always defend Lizzie against lies "made against her in public print and by gossiping persons who seem to delight in saying cruel things about her."[155]

LIFE AFTER EMMA

THE EARLY YEARS of the twentieth century brought several changes for Lizzie. Along with separating from her sister for good, Lizzie decided to change her name. Lizzie was her given name at birth, but around 1904 she changed it to Lizbeth. No one today knows why she chose that name, but "Lizzie A. Borden" never appeared again in the yearly directory of Fall River residents.

In the years after Emma left, Lizzie often developed close ties with her servants and their families. One of her closest relationships was with her housekeeper Hannah Nelson. Through her, Lizzie also became friends with Amanda Thelen. Lizzie was very upset when Hannah died in 1908. Writing to Amanda after the death, Lizzie said, "No one knows how I miss my Hannah."[156]

Lizzie also made changes to Maplecroft, though with Emma's permission. The sisters were still co-owners of the house. In 1909 Lizzie built a two-story addition and then a separate one-story addition. With the second addition, she had the name of her house carved into one of the new granite steps she had installed. William Savoie helped with the building of the stone steps. He later remembered Lizzie as "a great person to work for." And like some other people who met her in the years after the murder, Savoie thought "she was too nice a lady to have committed such a horrible crime."[157]

Two years after adding on to Maplecroft, Lizzie had a garage built for her car. Cars slowly became more common in Fall River during the first decade of the century. She had bought the land for the garage nine years before from her neighbors. At some point, she bought a second car. Over the years, she hired several chauffeurs to drive her around town. She became particularly close to Norman Hall and his family. Even after Hall no longer worked for her, Lizzie bought his children gifts and read to them when she visited them.

While Lizzie made new friends with her hired help and tried to live a quiet life, some people still remained fascinated with her and the murder of her parents. When the twentieth anniversary of her trial came, the *Boston Sunday Herald* wrote a story that described Lizzie's life in Fall River. The article later appeared in other papers. It tried to paint Lizzie as completely alone and cut off from any social life, which was not true. "After twenty years," the article said, "Lizzie Borden lives as shut off from the world as if she were behind prison bars." The article noted how the *Fall River Daily Globe* still published a story about the murders on their anniversary. "But if the woman ever sees them or hears of them, she has made no sign."[158] Around the time the *Herald* article appeared, the *Boston Sunday Post* published its interview with Emma. In it, Emma dismissed the stories about her father being so cheap that he had not fed his daughters properly.

During the anniversary year of 1913, Emma returned to Fall River, but she kept her promise not to live with Lizzie again. The sisters, though, still owned rental property together, including the house at 92 Second Street. In 1919 Lizzie and Emma finally sold the house where their parents were murdered. The sale ended Lizzie's direct tie to the family's horrible past.

14

THE END OF LIZZIE BORDEN

Through the 1910s and into the twenties, Lizzie continued to try to live a quiet life. If she made fewer trips to Fall River shops, she was a frequent visitor to Oak Grove Cemetery, where Andrew was buried, along with Alice, the sister who died before Lizzie was born. Abby was buried there too, and her name appears on the ten-foot-tall granite monument that Emma and Lizzie had placed on the gravesite in 1895. So does the name of Sarah Borden, Lizzie's mother.

Whether she's actually at the site, though, is in question. Borden murder scholar Stefani Koorey said that her research shows that Sarah was never moved to Oak Grove from her original burial spot at another cemetery.

On her trips to visit the graves, Lizzie often walked with Terrance Lomax, who was in charge of maintaining the grounds at the cemetery. Over the years he and Lizzie became friendly, and as they walked, Lomax told her to ignore people in the cemetery who turned to stare at her. As a young man, Lomax had gone to New Bedford to watch Lizzie's trial. In his later years, he felt sorry for her and all she'd had to endure. After they walked through the cemetery, Lizzie would sometimes try to give him money, but he always refused. And in the winters, Lizzie would call before she came to visit the family graves, and Lomax would shovel a path for her through any ice and snow on the grounds.

Lizzie traveled much farther when she made trips to one of her favorite cities, Washington, DC. For many years she had a cousin there, as well as several good friends. She saw the capital city as a place where she could rest when she got tired or upset with life's challenges. On some visits she would stay for a month.

When Lizzie went to Washington, she often went during the spring, when the city's famous cherry trees bloomed. In 1920 she sent a postcard of the blooming trees to her friend Amanda Thelen. She had stayed close with Amanda and her family since they had met through Hannah Nelson years before. She was particularly fond of Amanda's two daughters, Olga and Anna, who always knew Lizzie as "Auntie Borden."[159]

In her later years, Lizzie developed close relations with other children she came to know through her hired help at Maplecroft. In 1919 she hired Ernest Terry as her chauffeur, and he and his wife soon had a baby boy named Alden. Two years later, the Terrys had a daughter named Grace. Both children came to call Lizzie Auntie Borden too, and Lizzie had an especially strong bond with Alden. She often mailed him cards and notes. On at least one occasion, she went on a picnic with the Terry family, and sometimes she would join them on trips to a nearby town for ice cream.

TROUBLES AT HOME

AS LIZZIE'S NOTES from Washington revealed, she often went to the city when facing difficult times at home. One of those times came in 1923, when a fire broke out in the A. J. Borden building. Seven years earlier an even larger fire had swept through downtown Fall River, and that blaze also touched property the sisters owned. In each case, their properties suffered damage valued at between $16,000 and $20,000.

Shortly after the 1923 fire, Emma moved out of Fall River and settled in Newmarket, New Hampshire. In that small town away from Fall River, people did not seem to associate her with the once-famous murder of her parents and her sister's trial.

The mystery of the Borden murders, though, still fascinated some people. One of them was Edmund L. Pearson. A librarian, he was also a writer, and he was especially interested in true-crime stories. In 1923 he visited Fall River to do research on the Borden case. Before and after the visit, he exchanged letters with Frank Knowlton, the son of prosecutor Hosea Knowlton. The younger Knowlton helped Pearson meet people who knew something about Lizzie or the trial and let the author read his father's papers.

In November 1923 Pearson wrote to Knowlton about his visit. He described how he sat in his car outside Maplecroft for about thirty minutes. He realized the chances of actually seeing Lizzie emerge from the house were slim, but he was still disappointed when it didn't happen. He also went to a local store and asked if it sold pictures of 92 Second Street. The clerk said no and declared that "only 'outsiders' take any interest in the case."[160] Spending time in Fall River and talking to some of the residents, Pearson was convinced that many still believed that Lizzie had killed her parents—a view he shared.

The next year Pearson published *Studies in Murder*, a look at five famous killings. The Borden case was the first one he presented, spending 120 pages on it. Pearson wrote that the case was a "mysterious crime in a class of society where deeds of violence are not only foreign, but usually wildly impossible."[161] While Borden scholars don't know if Lizzie read the book,

Pearson claimed she had, though he didn't explain how he knew this. It's likely, though, that Lizzie knew about the book and the views Pearson presented about her guilt. The bookstore she often visited refused to carry the book, and so did the public library for several years. But by April 1926 the book was available there and was always in demand by Fall River residents.

In 1925, the year after *Studies in Murder* appeared, at least one friend sensed that Lizzie's health was starting to fail. In early 1926 her doctor suggested that Lizzie have surgery, possibly to have her gall bladder removed. She entered Truesdale Hospital in Fall River under the fake name of Mary Smith Borden. Just before the surgery, she drew up a will.

Even with the false name, however, some reporters caught wind that Lizzie was in the hospital. Her car was well known, and people often saw it there. She spent more than three weeks there after the surgery, then hired a nurse to live with her when she returned to Maplecroft. By the spring of 1927 Lizzie felt well enough to travel to Boston to see a play. But soon after that trip, her health began to fail.

THE DEATHS OF THE BORDEN SISTERS

IN MAY 1927 Lizzie called for her family doctor, who spent several days checking in on her. Lizzie, though, knew she was nearing the end of her life. As death approached, she gave Ernest Terry a check so he could make repairs to his house. Then, on the evening of June 1, Lizzie died. Her doctor said the cause was heart disease, with a lung infection adding to her health problems.

The newspapers hadn't learned that Lizzie was so ill, but on June 2 her doctor made news of her death public. The papers reported the facts of her death and then reminded readers of her parents' murder and the trial she faced afterward. The people closest to her had little to say publicly about her. The *Boston Globe* reported the comments of an unnamed friend who had told Lizzie that she should leave Fall River, since so many people had turned against her. Lizzie told the friend, "When the truth comes out about this murder, I want to be living here so I can walk down town and meet those of my old friends who have been cutting me all these years."[162]

Besides leaving a will, Lizzie had written instructions for her funeral service and burial. The service would feature the reading of several passages from the Bible and a poem and the singing of the song "My Ain Countrie." The funeral, she wrote, should be "strictly private with a short prayer at the grave."[163] She requested that she be buried at her father's feet. Lizzie also wanted to have a local Episcopal minister perform the service, not one from Central Congregational Church. She had never returned to Central after her treatment by the other members there. Helen Leighton, who had gotten to know Lizzie through the Fall River Animal Rescue League, recalled after the funeral how the women of the church "turned away from her and men whom she had known for years passed her without a word of greeting." Speaking to the *Fall River Herald*, Leighton wanted local people to know that Lizzie had about a dozen close friends who remained loyal over the years, and Lizzie "bestowed many, many kindnesses upon her friends" and "gave away thousands of dollars to aid needy causes which came to her attention."[164]

Among other good deeds, Lizzie bought books to give to poor residents who couldn't afford their own.

Lizzie was buried at Oak Grove Cemetery on June 4. Only a few of her close friends were there. One person who wasn't was Emma Borden. She had been sick for some time and couldn't leave New Hampshire to attend the funeral. On June 10 Emma died too. Her body was first taken to Swansea for a service, and then she was buried at the family plot in Fall River. Stories about her death always referred back to the family murders, Lizzie's trial, and the sisters' later separation.

With the sisters' deaths, the newspapers took an interest in their wealth and who would get their money. While some papers guessed that Lizzie was probably worth close to $1 million, in reality her estate was worth just over $300,000. Emma died even richer, with an estate worth almost $450,000. Reporting on her death, one paper noted that Emma had lived a simple lifestyle, and she had kept to herself after her move to New Hampshire.

Lizzie specifically did not include Emma in her will, writing that her sister "has her share of her father's estate and is supposed to have enough to make her comfortable." Lizzie left $30,000 and some stock to the Fall River Animal Rescue League, saying, "I have been fond of animals and their need is great and there are so few who care for them."[165] Lizzie left another $10,000 and some property to Charles Cook, who had managed her business affairs, and smaller amounts to several cousins, old friends, and employees. Chauffeur Ernest Terry and his family collected $6,000 as well as some property. As outlined in an earlier agreement with Emma, Maplecroft passed to her sister; the house then became part of her estate when she died.

In her will, Emma also gave money to organizations that helped animals and to other charities. These included the Girl Scouts and several groups that helped children in Fall River. Emma was generous with several friends and gave money to relatives, too.

Lizzie's death led to renewed interest in her life and the killing of her parents. To Frank Knowlton, some of the interest came from the recent publishing of Edmund L. Pearson's *Studies in Murder* and the focus it put on the case. Knowlton wrote Pearson to express that view, and he said that he believed Emma knew the truth of Lizzie's guilt. Knowlton wrote that not knowing Emma would die just a few days later. Knowlton, convinced that Lizzie was guilty, noted that her grave "has been dug beside the graves of her victims. May she rest in peace."[166]

Lizzie's body may have come to an end with her death, but the effort to solve the mystery of the Borden killings and place the blame on Lizzie never did.

15

KEEPING THE STORY ALIVE

On the day of the murders in 1892, Edwin Porter of the *Fall River Daily Globe* was on the scene. He followed the case through Lizzie's trial, and even before it started, he had come up with the name of the book he wanted to write: *The Fall River Tragedy: A History of the Borden Murders*. Like others who wrote about Lizzie and the murders, Porter believed Lizzie was guilty. But despite his bias the book he published just two months after the trial ended still provides valuable information about what took place in Fall River in 1892 and 1893.

Porter's book was the first in print about the murders. In his introduction, he summed up why the case fascinated people in 1893—and why it still fascinates many today. Lizzie was a woman of "spotless reputation and character" with strong ties to a local church. "Her arrest added more and more to the interest which the public had taken in the matter." Lizzie's trial settled her guilt, as far as the law was concerned, "yet the case lost none of its absorbing interest."[167] Porter stressed that his facts came from official sources and court records.

Even before the book's publication, Lizzie and Emma threatened to sue the publisher if it included "any false statement or colorable description."[168] After the book was published, rumors spread that Lizzie had bought, or at least tried to buy, all the copies so no one could see it. But some copies were sold, and the book was reprinted in 1985.

Shortly after Porter's book appeared, another one about the trial was published. *The Mystery Unveiled: The Truth About the Borden Tragedy* by Todd Lunday argued that the state and the police had gotten it right and Lizzie was guilty. Lunday was actually Cyrus

Daniel Harp, a minister in the Methodist church. It's not clear why he wrote so strongly about his belief in Lizzie's guilt.

For many years the *Fall River Daily Globe* kept Lizzie's story alive with its annual feature on the anniversary of the murders. Then Edmund Pearson published his *Studies in Murder*, and the case received national attention again. Pearson followed that with two other books that featured the Borden case. Then, in 1937, ten years after the Borden sisters' deaths, Pearson published *The Trial of Lizzie Borden*. His work helped sway public opinion against Lizzie.

MANY DIFFERENT THEORIES

OVER THE DECADES, more articles and books began to appear, arguing either for or against Lizzie's guilt. A 1943 book of true crime stories contained an article that said Lizzie accidentally killed her father after killing Abby. Ten years later Charles and Louise Samuels published *The Girl in the House of Hate*, which presented the facts of the case. In 1967 Virginia Lincoln, who had lived on the Hill, wrote her account of Lizzie and the murders. In *A Private Disgrace: Lizzie Borden by Daylight*, Lincoln argued that Lizzie was guilty, but she had a medical excuse. Lincoln claimed she suffered from a form of epilepsy, and when she had seizures she could do things she normally wouldn't do, such as shoplift—or kill her stepmother. Lincoln argued that Lizzie was thinking about killing Abby, but the ax murder was an unplanned attack stirred by one of her seizures.

Most scholars dismiss Lincoln's theory about Lizzie's seizures. Experts on the Borden case also reject other theories about who the killer was. Authors of different books and articles have suggested that Emma Borden, Bridget Sullivan, John Morse, and Dr. Seabury Bowen were all possible murderers of Andrew and Abby Borden. Another theory is that a man named David Anthony wanted to marry Lizzie, but Andrew opposed the wedding, so Anthony killed both Bordens.

THE UNKNOWN SON

In 1991 Arnold R. Brown introduced a new character in the Borden story. In *Lizzie Borden: The Legend, the Truth, the Final*

Chapter, he claimed that someone who knew the Bordens told him that Andrew Borden had a son outside of his two marriages named William S. Borden. The son learned that Andrew was not going to include him in his will and so set off to kill his father. William then confessed his crime to the source Brown used to write his book. Brown also asserted that Lizzie knew her alleged half brother had committed the murders and agreed to stand trial for his crime, hoping to get her inheritance early. The book said that both the prosecution and the defense knew the truth too and worked together to hide the real killer's identity. Lizzie supposedly used some of her wealth to buy the cooperation of local officials involved in the case. Brown has little evidence to support some of his claims, but some people still accept the possibility that Borden had a son and that he did the deed.

When not trying to show that other people committed the murders, various authors have argued why Lizzie could not have done them. One common argument is that she didn't have the time to murder both Abby and Andrew and then get rid of any bloody clothes and the murder weapon without being caught. Others say that whatever disagreements she had with her mother, they were not strong enough to lead a basically decent person to commit murder. Those who think Lizzie was the murderer stress, as the prosecution did, Lizzie's bad relations with Abby. These people say that Abby was her real target, and she murdered Andrew only when he came home unexpectedly early.

Some people convinced of Lizzie's guilt also point out her desire to live a life of greater luxury than her father allowed. But in recent decades, others have suggested that deeper forces of evil were at work in the Borden home, and Lizzie could not stand them anymore. While not offering concrete proof, several writers have suggested that Lizzie could have been the victim of physical abuse by her father, and that Abby knew about it and didn't try to stop it. If that were true, then Lizzie would have had an even better reason to kill both her parents.

LOOKING AT THE LEGAL ASPECTS

AS SOON AS the trial ended, several legal experts in Massachusetts wrote about how the justices handled the case. To former judge Charles G. Davis and law professor John Wigmore, the justices had failed to do their job properly. Both men wrote that the justices had failed to follow usual legal proceedings when they refused Knowlton's efforts to introduce Lizzie's inquest testimony. Whatever the mayor told Lizzie about being a suspect, she was in fact not under arrest. She volunteered to appear at the inquest—because Andrew Jennings thought it would help her case. Wigmore argued that the ruling on the inquest testimony let Jennings have things both ways: "to go on the stand when there was something to gain and to remain silent when the testimony proved dangerous to use."[169]

Davis also argued that Justice Dewey's charge to the jury went too far in arguing points that helped the defense. Dewey, Davis wrote, told the jury to "distrust every important item of evidence offered by the prosecution in the case."[170] With those instructions, and the difficulty in believing that a woman like Lizzie could commit such a horrible crime, it's not surprising the jury would rule in her favor.

Writing decades later, another legal expert made similar arguments. In 1974 Robert Sullivan wrote *Goodbye Lizzie Borden*. Sullivan was a former Massachusetts superior court justice and looked closely at the legal details of the case. Sullivan said that Justice Dewey's belief in Lizzie's innocence "shone unmistakably through the words of his instructions."[171] He wrote that most legal experts of Dewey's era thought the court should have let the state present the inquest testimony and the testimony that Lizzie tried to buy poison the day before the murders.

Another modern legal perspective came in 1989, with a new edition of Edmund L. Pearson's *The Trial of Lizzie Borden*. Noted lawyer Alan Dershowitz wrote an introduction for the book and argued that Lizzie had several advantages in the courtroom. One, as others have pointed out, was her social standing in Fall River. If Lizzie had been an Irish maid, like Bridget Sullivan, she most likely would have been found guilty, based on the evidence the prosecution presented. Instead Lizzie was a Yankee from a respectable family with deep roots in the city. Her other main advantage was the judges being so generous toward her and her lawyers in excluding evidence.

Dershowitz noted that law students have sometimes re-created the case as part of their class work. Given the evidence that was presented, many have argued that the state did not prove her guilt beyond a reasonable doubt. But a key point is that the evidence left out may have been enough to sway a modern jury, if not the all-male jury of farmers and craftsmen of 1893. Dershowitz ended his piece by stating that juries must make decisions based on the evidence they are allowed to hear. But they don't decide historical truth. "The Lizzie Borden case is an excellent example of divergence between the verdict of the jury and the verdict of history."[172]

LIZZIE IN ART

IN THE YEARS after Lizzie's death, artists of all kinds used the story of the Borden murders for inspiration. In some cases, they took the basic facts of the story and changed the name or the setting. That happened with *Nine Pine Street*, a 1934 play by John Colton and Carlton Miles. Their play is set in New Bedford, with one of two sisters in the family killing their parents. Another play, Lillian de la Torre's *Goodbye, Miss Lizzie Borden: A Sinister Play in One Act*, makes Emma the murderer, with Lizzie taking the blame for her crime. Later plays have included *Blood Relations*. First staged in 1981, this play by Sharon Pollock has one character ask Lizzie if she murdered her parents. The questioner then adds, "If you say yes, I'll be horrified; if you say no, I'll be disappointed."[173] Lizzie's story has also been the subject of operas, ballets, movies, and one popular comic song. In 1961 the Chad Mitchell Trio released "You Can't Chop Your Papa Up in Massachusetts," which included the lines, "Some folks say she didn't do it, and others say of course she did/But they all agree Miss Lizzie B. was a problem kind of kid."[174]

In some of the fictional stories, the creators give Lizzie a lover, who becomes central to her reason for killing. Most of the stories, Professor Ann Schofield has noted, usually take one of two forms: a love story, or a story about a woman seeking freedom and independence during the rigid Victorian era. Some of the stories explore sexual themes, suggesting that Lizzie had female lovers or even had sexual relations with her father. Clearly, the artists go beyond the known facts of the case, working in rumors or their own inventions.

Some female writers see the story through a feminist view. Feminism had its roots in the late eighteenth century and maintains that women should be treated the same as men. Feminist artists explored the way a society dominated by men tried to limit what women could do for work and in their social lives. Lizzie's story provided a framework for exploring feminism and the problems women faced through the twentieth century and still face today. For Sharon Pollock, writing about Lizzie was a way to deal with the physical abuse she suffered when she was married. Pollock once said, "I would have killed to maintain my sense of self. . . . And so it was with Lizzie."[175]

The artistic interest in Lizzie has remained strong in recent years. In 2009 New York's Living Theater staged the rock musical *Lizzie Borden*. In reviewing the piece, the *New York Times* said the show had elements of humor, and one of the high points was "Why Are All These Heads Off?" a song about the pigeons that lost their heads weeks before the Borden murders. Two years later a play considered one of the most accurate fictional accounts of the story played in Fall River. Garrett Heater, the writer of *Lizzie Borden Took an Axe*, said his play was meant to appeal to both people who knew many details about the case and those who didn't. And unlike many artists, he didn't take a stand on whether or not Lizzie was guilty.

In 2014 a TV movie used the same title as Heater's play. But in this version of the story, there's no doubt that Lizzie was the murderer. Christina Ricci played Lizzie and repeated the role the next year in a miniseries called *The Lizzie Borden Chronicles*.

THE INTEREST—AND MYSTERY—REMAIN

ON THE INTERNET, several websites are devoted to Lizzie, the Borden murders, and the ongoing efforts to learn the truth about the case. New books and reissues of old ones come out every year.

Visitors can stay in the house where Abby and Andrew Borden were hacked to death. The house is now a bed-and-breakfast, and on the anniversary of the killings, actors play the parts of Lizzie, Bridget, and others involved in the murders and the trial that followed.

For fans of the case, one of the most interesting developments came in 2012. The Fall River Historical Society announced that a relative of Andrew Jennings had donated the lawyer's personal notes from his defense of Lizzie. The donation also included articles Jennings cut out of the newspapers after the murders.

The historical society has the largest collection of information on Lizzie and the murders. Its curators, Michael Martins and Dennis A. Binette, had already written the massive *Parallel Lives* about Lizzie and Fall River during her lifetime. They had the job of going through Jennings's papers and preparing transcripts for the public. By early 2017, the society had not released the entire contents of what it received. Binette said the papers were in bad shape and Jennings's handwriting was difficult to read. But he was sure that there was no "smoking gun"; Jennings believed in Lizzie's innocence, and his writings reflect that.[176]

What the papers do show is that Abby Borden's body was moved once it was discovered. Jennings took down the words of Charles Sawyer, the local man who stood guard at the side door on August 4, 1892. He had been in Abby's room and saw her body moved from under the bed. And it seemed to Sawyer that Abby had seen her attacker before he or she killed her, and that Abby tried to escape. Does that mean the attacker was a stranger? Would Abby have run if she saw Lizzie enter the room? Or could Abby have seen Lizzie carrying the hatchet and realized what was going to happen? After all, she already thought that someone was trying to poison her.

Students of the Borden murders eagerly await the release of all of Jennings's papers. Even if his notes don't contain a smoking gun, they will provide more details about one of the most famous unsolved murders in history. Some people today, of course, don't need more proof—they believe Lizzie brutally murdered her parents on that muggy August morning. Others say that the animal-loving, generous "Auntie Borden" could never have committed the crime.

What do you think?

MURDERER IN THE FAMILY?

Jim Fallon is a California scientist who studies the brain. He also has some distant relatives—including Lizzie Borden—who were or might have been murderers. Fallon has studied the brains of living psychopaths, people who have violent tendencies they can't control. He and other scientists have identified parts of the brain that are not well developed in psychopaths. This could explain their violent tendencies. After learning about the violence in his family tree, Fallon took high-tech images of his own brain—and discovered that it is similar to the brains of the psychopaths. He also took samples of his and living relatives' DNA. The chemicals that form DNA shape a person's physical appearance and some of their character traits. Fallon learned that he has a gene, part of DNA, that can make someone prone to violence. He is not a violent person, despite having that gene and the brain scan similar to a psychopath's. But there is evidence that the brain may affect someone's tendencies toward violence, and that trait could be passed down from one generation to the next.

Also important, however, is whether someone was the target of violence or abuse early in their lives.

So did Fallon's relative Lizzie have the same brain and DNA he does? We'll never know. But if she was a murderer, her own body may have set her on that path. And the true, hidden relationships among the members of her family may have played a role as well.

ACKNOWLEDGMENTS

My deepest thanks to Dennis A. Binette of the Fall River Historical Society for his expertise and patience.

TIME LINE

September 13, 1822	Andrew J. Borden is born.
December 26, 1845	Andrew Borden marries Sarah Anthony Morse.
March 1, 1851	Emma Lenora Boren is born.
May 3, 1856	Alice Esther Borden is born.
March 10, 1858	Alice Borden dies.
July 19, 1860	Lizzie Andrew Borden is born.
March 26, 1863	Sarah Borden dies.
June 6, 1865	Andrew Borden marries Abby Durfee Gray.
October 1, 1887	Andrew Borden gives his daughters a house on Ferry Street.
Summer 1890	Lizzie Borden takes an eleven-week tour of Europe with friends.
June 1891	Daylight robbery in the Borden house.

July 15, 1892	Andrew Borden repurchases the Ferry Street house from his daughters.
August 3, 1892	Andrew and Abby Borden are sick at midnight.
	John Morse arrives.
	Lizzie Borden calls on Alice Russell.
August 4, 1892	
7:00 a.m.	Andrew and Abby Borden eat breakfast with John Morse.
8:45 a.m.	John Morse leaves the Borden house.
8:50 a.m.	Lizzie Borden comes down for breakfast alone.
9:15 a.m.	Andrew Borden goes downtown for a shave.
9:30 a.m.	Abby Borden is murdered in the guest room.

10:45 a.m.	Andrew Borden returns, not feeling well.
11:05 a.m.	Lizzie Borden tells the maid that Andrew Borden has been killed.
11:30 a.m.	John Morse returns.
August 6, 1892	Funeral of Andrew and Abby Borden.
August 11, 1892	Lizzie Borden is arrested.
August 12, 1892	Lizzie is arraigned in district court and transferred to Taunton Jail.
September 1, 1892	Hearing in district court before Judge Blaisdell. Lizzie is held for grand jury.
November 15–21, 1892	Grand jury.
December 1, 1892	Alice Russell appears before the grand jury.
December 2, 1892	Indictments are delivered against Lizzie Borden for both murders.

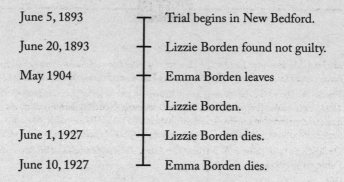

June 5, 1893	Trial begins in New Bedford.
June 20, 1893	Lizzie Borden found not guilty.
May 1904	Emma Borden leaves Lizzie Borden.
June 1, 1927	Lizzie Borden dies.
June 10, 1927	Emma Borden dies.

NOTES

1. Michael Martins and Dennis A. Binette, *Parallel Lives: A Social History of Lizzie A. Borden and Her Fall River* (Fall River, MA: Fall River Historical Society, 2010), 18.

2. Frank H. Burt, *Official Stenographic Report of the Trial of Lizzie Andrew Borden, 1893*, two vols. (Prepared by Harry Widdows, 2003. Available online at http://lizzieandrewborden.com/wp-content/uploads/2011/12/TrialBorden1.pdf and http://lizzieandrewborden.com/wp-content/uploads/2011/12/TrialBorden2.pdf), vol. I, 240.

3. David Kent and Robert A. Flynn. *The Lizzie Borden Sourcebook* (Boston: Branden Publishing, 1992), 83.

4. *Ibid.*

5. *Preliminary Hearing, Commonwealth of Massachusetts v. Lizzie Borden, Thursday, August 25, 1892 Thru Thursday, September 1, 1892*, five vols. (Prepared by Faye Musselman, 2001), 271.

6. *The Lizzie Borden Sourcebook*, 88.

7. *Ibid.*, 1.

8. Joseph A. Conforti, *Lizzie Borden on Trial: Murder, Ethnicity, and Gender* (Lawrence: University Press of Kansas, 2015), 70–71.

9. *The Lizzie Borden Sourcebook*, 4.

10. Olive Woolley Burt, *American Murder Ballads* (New York: Oxford University Press, 1958), 14.

11. Henry Milne Fenner, *History of Fall River, Massachusetts* (Fall River, MA: Fall River Merchants Association, 1911), 18.

12. *Parallel Lives*, 12.

13. Victoria Lincoln, *A Private Disgrace: Lizzie Borden by Daylight* (East Sandwich, MA: Seraphim Press, 2012), 19.

14. *Lizzie Borden on Trial*, 32.

15. *Parallel Lives*, 59.

16. *Ibid.*, 60.

17. *Ibid.*, 61.

18. *The Lizzie Borden Sourcebook*, 57.

19. "The Borden Mansion Empty," *New York Times*, September 10, 1893, 12.

20. *Parallel Lives*, 94.

21. *The Lizzie Borden Sourcebook*, 133.

22. *Parallel Lives*, 226.

23. *Ibid.*, 228.

24. *Ibid.*, 240.

25. *The Lizzie Borden Sourcebook*, 91.

26. *Parallel Lives*, 40.

27. *Ibid.*, 386.

28. Burt, *The Trial of Lizzie Andrew Borden*, vol. II, 1169.

29. *Lizzie Borden on Trial*, 49.

30. Burt, *The Trial of Lizzie Andrew Borden*, vol. I, 376.

31. *Ibid.*, 377.

32. *Ibid.*

33. *Ibid.*, 378.

34. *Preliminary Hearing*, 355.

35. *Ibid.*, 356–357.

36. *Parallel Lives*, 31.

37. *The Lizzie Borden Sourcebook*, 10.

38. *Ibid.*

39. Arthur Sherman Phillips, "The Borden Murder Mystery: In Defence of Lizzie Borden," 2. Abstract from *The Phillips History of Fall River*, prepared by Stefani Koorey, 2002. Available online at http://lizzieandrewborden.com/wp-content/uploads/2011/12/PhillipsBook.pdf.

40. *Parallel Lives*, 408.

41. *The Lizzie Borden Sourcebook*, 16.

42. *Ibid.*

43. *Lizzie Borden on Trial*, 76.

44. *Ibid.*, 77.

45. Burt, *The Trial of Lizzie Andrew Borden*, vol. II, 1162–1163.

46. *Ibid.*, 1163.

47. *The Lizzie Borden Sourcebook*, 17.

48. *Ibid.*, 27.

49. *Ibid.*, 25.

50. *Parallel Lives*, 38.

51. *Lizzie Borden on Trial*, 81.

52. *The Lizzie Borden Sourcebook*, 37.

53. Edwin H. Porter, *The Fall River Tragedy* (Fall River, MA: J. D. Munroe, 1893). Available online at http://lizzieandrewborden.com/wp-content/uploads/2011/12/FallRiverTrag.pdf), 52–53.

54. *The Lizzie Borden Sourcebook*, 38.

55. *Ibid.*, 56.

56. *Ibid.*

57. *Ibid.*, 66.

58. *Ibid.*, 81.

59. *Ibid.*, 102.

60. *Ibid.*, 50–51.

61. *Ibid.*, 105.

62. *Ibid.*, 104.

63. *The Fall River Tragedy*, 76.

64. *Lizzie Borden on Trial*, 102.

65. *The Lizzie Borden Sourcebook*, 115.

66. *Ibid.*, 127.

67. *Ibid.*, 131.

68. *Ibid.*

69. "The Borden Murder Mystery: In Defence of Lizzie Borden," i.

70. *Ibid.*, 14.

71. *The Lizzie Borden Sourcebook*, 136.

72. *The Fall River Tragedy*, 86.

73. *Lizzie Borden on Trial*, 107.

74. *The Lizzie Borden Sourcebook*, 148.

75. *Ibid.*, 158.

76. *Preliminary Hearing*, 316–317.

77. *The Lizzie Borden Sourcebook*, 178.

78. *Ibid.*, 187.

79. *Preliminary Hearing*, 478.

80. *Lizzie Borden on Trial*, 114.

81. *The Fall River Tragedy*, 135.

82. *Ibid.*, 138.

83. *Lizzie Borden on Trial*, 117.

84. *The Lizzie Borden Sourcebook*, 197.

85. *Parallel Lives*, 480.

86. *Lizzie Borden on Trial*, 117.

87. "Mrs. Livermore's Opinion," *New York Times*, September 4, 1892, 5.

88. *Lizzie Borden on Trial*, 103.

89. *Ibid.*, 119.

90. *The Lizzie Borden Sourcebook*, 316.

91. "The Borden Stories Untrue," *New York Times*, October 12, 1892, 3.

92. *The Fall River Tragedy*, 142.

93. "The Jurymen Talk," *New York Times*, December 7, 1892, 3.

94. No title, *New York Times*, December 6, 1892, 3.

95. "The Jurymen Talk."

96. *Parallel Lives*, 483–484.

97. Michael Martins and Dennis A. Binette. *The Commonwealth of Massachusetts vs. Lizzie A. Borden: The Knowlton Papers, 1892–1893* (Fall River, MA: Fall River Historical Society 1994), 36–37, 40.

98. *Parallel Lives*, 485.

99. "Lizzie Borden Arraigned," *New York Times*, May 9, 1893, 2.

100. *Parallel Lives*, 487.

101. *Lizzie Borden on Trial*, 133.

102. *The Lizzie Borden Sourcebook*, 206.

103. "Borden Murder Trial Begun," *New York Times*, June 6, 1893, 2.

104. *The Lizzie Borden Sourcebook*, 205.

105. *Lizzie Borden on Trial*, 136.

106. *The Lizzie Borden Sourcebook*, 213, 215.

107. *Ibid.*, 213.

108. *Ibid.*, 219.

109. Linda Rodriguez McRobbie, "The Strange and Mysterious History of the Ouija Board," *Smithsonian*, October 27, 2013. Available online at http://www.smithsonian-mag.com/history/the-strange-and-mysterious-history-of-the-ouija-board-5860627/.

110. *Knowlton Papers*, 341.

111. *Lizzie Borden on Trial*, 147.

112. Burt, *The Trial of Lizzie Andrew Borden*, vol. I, 391, 393.

113. *The Lizzie Borden Sourcebook*, 251.

114. *Lizzie Borden on Trial*, 163.

115. *The Lizzie Borden Sourcebook*, 264.

116. Burt, *The Trial of Lizzie Andrew Borden*, vol. II, 1214.

117. *Ibid.*, 1318–1319.

118. *The Lizzie Borden Sourcebook*, 288.

119. *The Lizzie Borden Sourcebook*, 286.

120. Burt, *The Trial of Lizzie Andrew Borden*, vol. II, 1540.

121. "Ready for the Arguments," *New York Times*, June 17, 1893, 9.

122. *The Lizzie Borden Sourcebook*, 296.

123. Burt, *The Trial of Lizzie Andrew Borden*, vol. II, 1610, 1612.

124. *Ibid.*, 1748–1749.

125. *Ibid.*, 1752–1753.

126. *Ibid.*, 1758.

127. *Ibid.*, 1807.

128. *Ibid.*, 1869, 1882.

129. *Ibid.*, 1883.

130. *The Lizzie Borden Sourcebook*, 311.

131. Burt, *The Trial of Lizzie Andrew Borden*, vol. II, 1894.

132. *The Lizzie Borden Sourcebook*, 311.

133. Burt, *The Trial of Lizzie Andrew Borden*, vol. II, 1929.

134. *Parallel Lives*, 512.

135. *Ibid.*, 515.

136. "Miss Borden at Fall River," *New York Times*, June 21, 1893, 2.

137. *Ibid.*

138. *Parallel Lives*, 514.

139. *The Lizzie Borden Sourcebook*, 328.

140. *Parallel Lives*, 605.

141. *Parallel Lives*, 520.

142. *Lizzie Borden on Trial*, 209.

143. "The Acquittal of Miss Borden," *New York Times*, June 21, 1893, 4.

144. *Lizzie Borden on Trial*, 213.

145. *Parallel Lives*, 538.

146. *Ibid.*

147. *Ibid.*, 653–654.

148. Joyce Williams, J. Eric Smithburn, and Jeanne M. Peterson, *Lizzie Borden: A Case Book of Family and Crime in the 1890s* (Bloomington, IN: Tichenor Publishing, 1981), 262, 264.

149. *A Private Disgrace*, 6, 10.

150. *Parallel Lives*, 662.

151. *Ibid.*, 665.

152. *Ibid.*, 436.

153. *Ibid.*, 724.

154. *A Private Disgrace*, 299.

155. *Parallel Lives*, 741.

156. *Ibid.*, 773.

157. *Ibid.*, 781.

158. "Condemned by Public Opinion," *Fort Mill Times*, April 24, 1913, 6.

159. *Parallel Lives*, 839.

160. *Ibid.*, 959.

161. Amy Gilman Srebnick, "Pearson, Edmund Lester: *Studies in Murder*," *Crime, History & Societies*, vol. 5, no. 1 (2001), 145–146. Available online at https://chs.revues.org/797/.

162. *The Lizzie Borden Sourcebook*, 332.

163. *Parallel Lives*, 980.

164. *The Lizzie Borden Sourcebook*, 340.

165. *Ibid.*, 338.

166. *Parallel Lives*, 984.

167. *The Fall River Tragedy*, 2.

168. *Parallel Lives*, 527.

169. Edmund Pearson, *The Trial of Lizzie Borden*, prepared by Harry Widdows, 64. Available online at http://lizzieandrewborden.com/wp-content/uploads/2011/12/TrialLBPearson.pdf.

170. *Lizzie Borden on Trial*, 210.

171. Robert Sullivan, *Goodbye Lizzie Borden* (Brattleboro, VT: Stephen Greene Press, 1974), 172.

172. Edmund Pearson, *The Trial of Lizzie Borden*, introduction by Alan Dershowitz (Omaha: Gryphon Editions Notable Trials Library, 1989).

173. Ann Schofield, "Lizzie Borden Took an Axe: History, Feminism and American Culture." *American Studies*, vol. 34, no. 1 (Spring 1993), 92.

174. "Chad Mitchell Trio to Visit Lizzie Borden House," Lizzie Borden: Warps & Wefts, September 6, 2010, https://lizziebordenwarpsandwefts.com/2010/09/06/chad-mitchell-trio-to-visit-lizzie-borden-house/.

175. "Lizzie Borden Took an Axe," 96.

176. Interview with Dennis A. Binette, September 30, 2016.

FURTHER READING

BOOKS

Anderson, Jennifer Joline. *Women's Rights Movement*. Minneapolis: ABDO Publishing Company, 2014.

Hepplewhite, Peter. *Men, Women and Children in Victorian Times*. London: Wayland, 2013.

Kent, David, and Robert A. Flynn. *The Lizzie Borden Sourcebook*. Boston: Branden Publishing, 1992.

Miller, Sarah Elizabeth. *The Borden Murders: Lizzie Borden & The Trial of the Century*. New York: Schwartz & Wade Books, 2016.

WEBSITES

FALL RIVER HISTORICAL SOCIETY http://www.fallriverhistorical.org/

LIZZIE BORDEN BED & BREAKFAST https://www.lizzie-borden.com/

LIZZIE BORDEN TRIAL http://famous-trials.com/lizzieborden/

LIZZIE BORDEN: WARPS & WEFTS https://lizziebordenwarpsandwefts.com/

THE LIZZIE ANDREW BORDEN VIRTUAL MUSEUM & LIBRARY http://lizzieandrewborden.com/

TATTERED FABRIC: FALL RIVER'S LIZZIE BORDEN https://phayemuss.wordpress.com/

SELECTED BIBLIOGRAPHY

Allard, Deborah. "Excerpts from Lawyer's Journal Reveal New Insight into Borden Case." *The Herald News*, August 2, 2013. Available online at http://www.heraldnews.com/x273444677/Excerpts-from-lawyers -journal-reveal-new-insight-into-Borden-case.

————. "Folks Flock to Fall River for Lizzie Anniversary." *South Coast Today*, August 4, 2016. Available online at http://www.southcoasttoday .com/article/20160804/NEWS/160809764.

Burt, Frank H. *Official Stenographic Report of the Trial of Lizzie Andrew Borden, 1893*. Two vols. Prepared by Harry Widdows, 2003. Available online at http://lizzieandrewborden.com/wp-content/uploads/2011 /12/TrialBorden1.pdf and http://lizzieandrewborden.com/wp-content /uploads/2011/12/TrialBorden2.pdf.

Burt, Olive Woolley. *American Murder Ballads*. New York: Oxford University Press, 1958.

"Chad Mitchell Trio to Visit Lizzie Borden House." Lizzie Borden: Warps & Wefts, September 6, 2010, https://lizziebordenwarpsandwefts .com/2010/09/06/chad-mitchell-trio-to-visit-lizzie-borden-house/.

Chapman, Sherry. *Lizzie Borden: Resurrections*. Fall River, MA: Pear Tree Press, 2014.

Conforti, Joseph A. *Lizzie Borden on Trial: Murder, Ethnicity, and Gender*. Lawrence: University Press of Kansas, 2015.

Cushman, Clare. *Supreme Court Justices: Illustrated Biographies*. Rev. ed. Washington, DC: CQ Press, 2012.

Fenner, Henry Milne. *History of Fall River, Massachusetts*. Fall River, MA: Fall River Merchants Association, 1911.

Genzlinger, Neil. "Rock on, Ax Murderer: 40 Whacks, Many Songs." *New York Times*, September 25, 2009. Available online at http://www.nytimes.com/2009/09/25/theater/reviews/25lizzie.html?_r=0.

Hagerty, Barbara Bradley. "A Neuroscientist Uncovers a Dark Secret." NPR, June 29, 2010. Available online at http://www.npr.org/templates/story/story.php?storyId=127888976.

Kent, David, and Robert A. Flynn. *The Lizzie Borden Sourcebook*. Boston: Branden Publishing, 1992.

Lincoln, Victoria. *A Private Disgrace: Lizzie Borden by Daylight*. East Sandwich, MA: Seraphim Press, 2012.

Martins, Michael, and Dennis A. Binette. *The Commonwealth of Massachusetts vs. Lizzie A. Borden: The Knowlton Papers, 1892–1893*. Fall River, MA: Fall River Historical Society, 1994.

—————. *Parallel Lives: A Social History of Lizzie A. Borden and Her Fall River*. Fall River, MA: Fall River Historical Society, 2010.

"New Lizzie Borden Play—Performances in Fall River." *Tattered Fabric: Fall River's Lizzie Borden*, June 29, 2011, https://phayemuss.wordpress.com/tag/garrett-heater/.

The Official Report of the Trial of Sarah Jane Robinson for the Murder of Prince Arthur Freeman: In the Supreme Judicial Court of Massachusetts. Boston: Wright & Potter Print Company, 1888.

Pearson, Edmund. *The Trial of Lizzie Borden*. Prepared by Harry Widdows. Available online at http://lizzieandrewborden.com/wp-content/uploads/2011/12/TrialLBPearson.pdf.

—————. *The Trial of Lizzie Borden*. Introduction by Alan Dershowitz. Omaha: Gryphon Editions Notable Trials Library, 1989.

Phillips, Arthur Sherman. "The Borden Murder Mystery: In Defence of Lizzie Borden." Abstract from *The Phillips History of Fall River*.

Prepared by Stefani Koorey, 2002. Available online at http://lizzie andrewborden.com/wp-content/uploads/2011/12/PhillipsBook.pdf.

Porter, Edwin H. *The Fall River Tragedy*. Fall River, MA: J. D. Munroe, 1893. Available online at http://lizzieandrewborden.com/wp-content /uploads/2011/12/FallRiverTrag.pdf.

Preliminary Hearing, Commonwealth of Massachusetts v. Lizzie Borden, Thursday, August 25, 1892 Thru Thursday, September 1, 1892. Five vols. Prepared by Faye Musselman, 2001. Robertson, Cara W. "Representing 'Miss Lizzie': Cultural Convictions in the Trial of Lizzie Borden." *Yale Journal of Law & the Humanities*, vol. 8, no. 2 (1996), 351–416.

Rodriguez McRobbie, Linda. "The Strange and Mysterious History of the Ouija Board." *Smithsonian*, October 27, 2013. Available online at http://www.smithsonianmag.com/history/the-strange-and-mysterious -history-of-the-ouija-board-5860627/.

Schofield, Ann. "Lizzie Borden Took an Axe: History, Feminism and American Culture." *American Studies*, vol. 34, no. 1 (Spring 1993), 91–103.

Srebnick, Amy Gilman. "Pearson, Edmund Lester: *Studies in Murder*." Crime, History & Societies, vol. 5, no. 1 (2001), 145–146. Available online at https://chs.revues.org/797/.

Sullivan, Robert. *Goodbye Lizzie Borden*. Brattleboro, VT: Stephen Greene Press, 1974.

Williams, Joyce, J. Eric Smithburn, and Jeanne M. Peterson. *Lizzie Borden: A Case Book of Family and Crime in the 1890s*. Bloomington, IN: Tichenor Publishing, 1981.

Yeshion, Ted. "The Myths of Circumstantial Evidence." *Forensic Teacher* magazine, http://www.theforensicteacher.com/Evidence.html.

ABOUT THE AUTHOR

Michael Burgan has written more than 250 books for children and young adults, both fiction and nonfiction. His works include biographies of US and world leaders and histories of the American Revolution, World War II, and the Cold War. A graduate of the University of Connecticut with a degree in history, Burgan is also a produced playwright and the editor of *The Biographer's Craft*, the newsletter of Biographers International Organization. He lives in Santa Fe, New Mexico, with his cat, Callie.

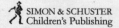